MACKINTOSH

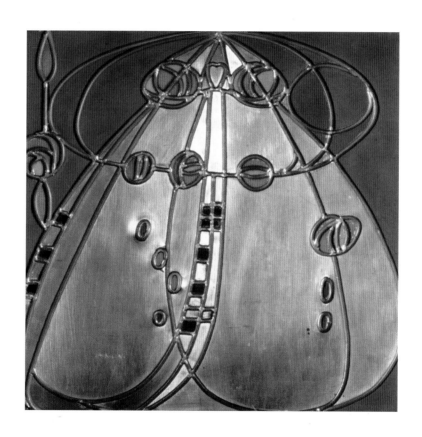

This edition published for
Lomond Books Ltd, Broxburn, EH52, Scotland. 2010

Produced by **FLAME TREE PUBLISHING**

Publisher and Creative Director: Nick Wells
Picture Research: Melinda Révész
Project Editor: Chelsea Edwards
Editor: Sarah Goulding
Designer: Mike Spender
Production: Chris Herbert
Proofreader: Dawn Laker
Indexer: Helen Snaith

Special thanks to: Polly Prior, Geoffrey Meadon, Sara Robson and Helen Tovey

FLAME TREE PUBLISHING

Crabtree Hall, Crabtree Lane
Fulham, London, SW6 6TY
United Kingdom

www.flametreepublishing.com

First published 2010

10 12 14 13 11

1 3 5 7 9 10 8 6 4 2

Flame Tree is part of the Foundry Creative Media Company Limited

© 2010 Flame Tree Publishing

ISBN 978 1 84204 217 5

A CIP record for this book is available from the British Library upon request.

Printed in China

MACKINTOSH

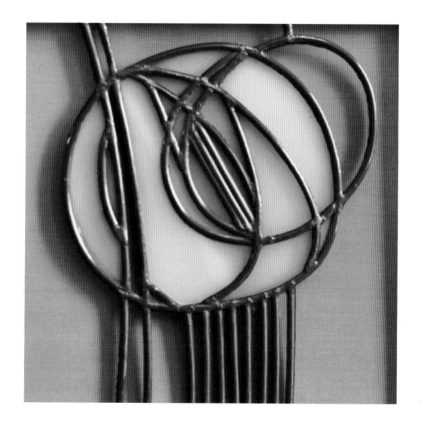

AUTHOR: TAMSIN PICKERAL

LOMOND

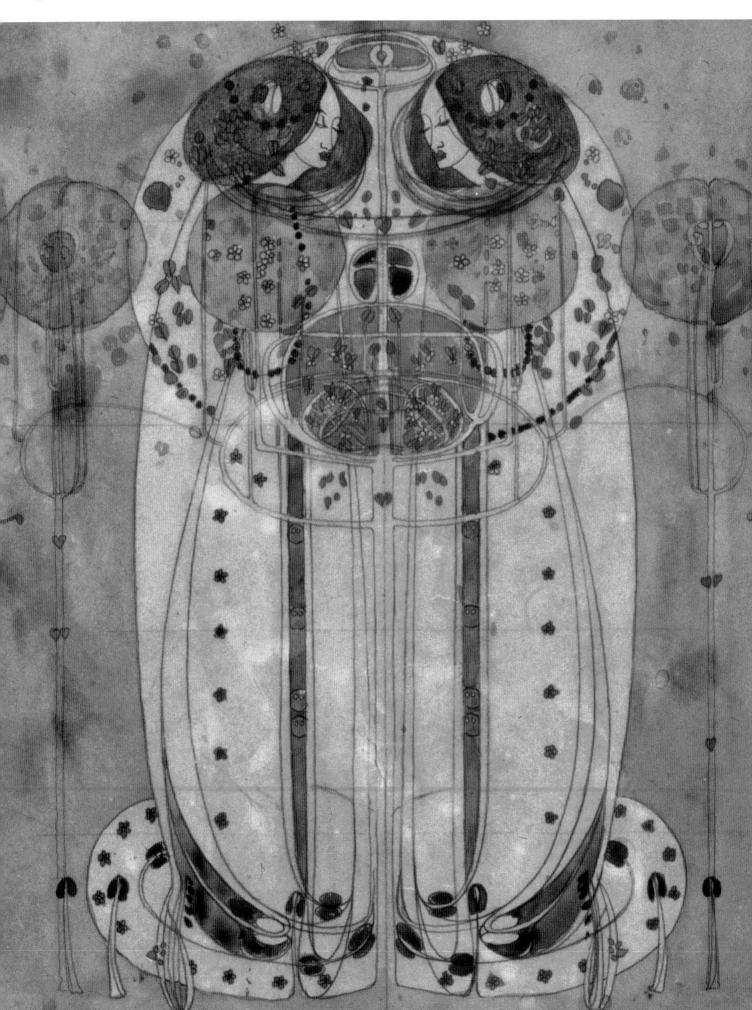

CONTENTS

HOW TO USE THIS BOOK 6

FOREWORD 8

INTRODUCTION 12

LIFE 18

SOCIETY 40

PLACES 54

INFLUENCES 74

STYLES & TECHNIQUES 100

AUTHOR BIOGRAPHIES AND PICTURE CREDITS 122

FURTHER READING 123

INDEX BY WORK 124

GENERAL INDEX 125

HOW TO USE THIS BOOK

The reader is encouraged to use this book in a variety of ways, each of which caters for a range of interests, knowledge and uses.

- The book is organized into five sections: **Life**, **Society**, **Places**, **Influences** and **Styles & Techniques**.

- **Life** provides a snapshot of how Mackintosh's work developed during the course of his career, showing the different media in which he worked.

- **Society** shows how Mackintosh's artefacts and designs reflect contemporaneous society, and how events of the time were a source of inspiration and frustration to him.

- **Places** looks at the work Mackintosh did in the different places he lived in and travelled to: Glasgow, Italy, London and France.

- **Influences** reveals Mackintosh's sources of inspiration, including the 'Group of Four', artistic movements including Arts and Crafts and Art Nouveau, and how much of his work anticipated Modernism.

- **Styles & Techniques** delves into the different techniques he used to produce his architectural designs as well as his furniture, textiles and paintings.

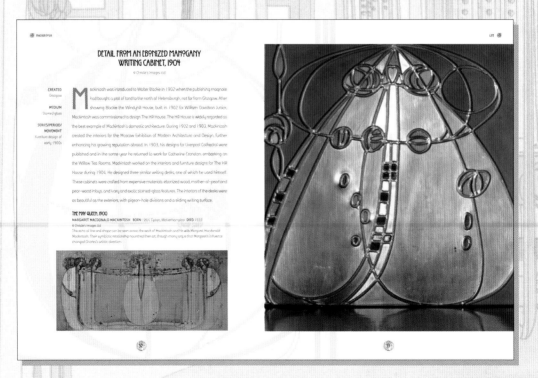

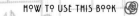

Title of work (NB: all works are by Mackintosh unless another artist's name is given at the side of the page)

Date of work (if known)

Picture credit

MACKINTOSH

DETAIL FROM AN EBONIZED MAHOGANY WRITING CABINET, 1904

© Christie's Images Ltd

Place in which the work was created (if known)

Medium in which the work was created (if known)

Series, period or movement to which the work belongs (if known)

CREATED
Glasgow

MEDIUM
Stained glass

**SERIES/PERIOD/
MOVEMENT**
Furniture design of
early 1900s

Mackintosh was introduced to Walter Blackie in 1902 when the publishing magnate had bought a plot of land to the north of Helensburgh, not far from Glasgow. After showing Blackie the Windyhill House, built in 1902 for William Davidson Junior, Mackintosh was commissioned to design The Hill House. The Hill House is widely regarded as the best example of Mackintosh's domestic architecture. During 1902 and 1903, Mackintosh created the interiors for the Moscow Exhibition of Modern Architecture and Design, further enhancing his growing reputation abroad. In 1903, his designs for Liverpool Cathedral were published and in the same year he returned to work for Catherine Cranston, embarking on the Willow Tea Rooms. Mackintosh worked on the interiors and furniture designs for The Hill House during 1904. He designed three similar writing desks, one of which he used himself. These cabinets were crafted from expensive materials: ebonized wood, mother-of-pearl and pear-wood inlays, and ivory and exotic stained-glass features. The interiors of the desks were as beautiful as the exteriors, with pigeon-hole divisions and a sliding writing surface.

Information about the work and the context within which it was created

Title of similar work (NB: all works are by Mackintosh unless another artist's name is given underneath the title.

THE MAY QUEEN, 1900
MARGARET MACDONALD MACKINTOSH BORN 1864 Tipton, Wolverhampton DIED 1933
© Christie's Images Ltd
The echo of line and shape can be seen across the work of Mackintosh and his wife Margaret Macdonald Mackintosh. Their symbiotic relationship nourished their art, though many argue that Margaret's influence changed Charles's artistic direction.

Picture credit

Similar work to the main one pictured

FOREWORD

'There are things more precious, more beautiful, more lasting than life.'
CHARLES RENNIE MACKINTOSH

E very biography ought to add to our knowledge of the subject. The problem with the straightforward chronological route, particularly when the subject is as artistically diverse as the Scottish architect Charles Rennie Mackintosh, is that generally you can explain everything except the bit that matters. The methodology of this particular approach is to examine his life, the society in which he lived, the places where he practised his profession, the sources from which his inspiration flowed and the styles and techniques he employed to express his individuality; then to scrutinize it further through examples of his work. It is far from the usual worthy but occasionally dry sequential progress. What is offered is an analytical survey that gives a rounder, truer notion of not only his artistic development, but the effects and influences of the extraordinary flourish that became known as the Glasgow Style: a biographical technique very much in line with Mackintosh's own belief that the artist '...depends very greatly for his success upon a kind of synthesis, an integration of myriads of details and circumstances'.

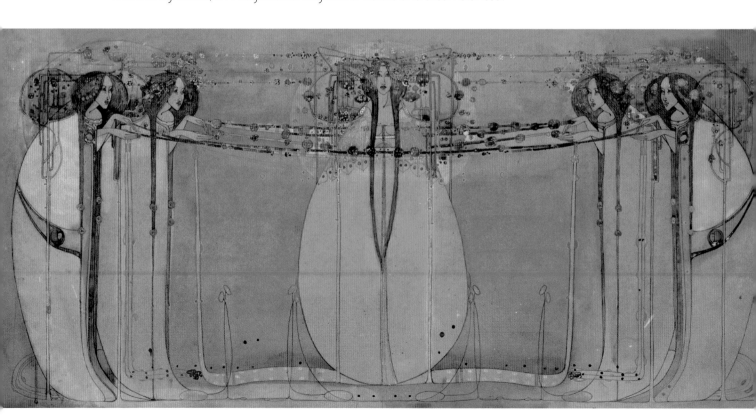

For every piece of work, there is a similar one with echoed elements also illustrated: points of comparison that illuminate the man and act as a benchmark for his progress. Learning, after all, is being able to see the relationship between things. The evolution of a unique artistic style is therefore traceable through distinct areas of influence, and as a consequence the aesthetic inheritance can be better assessed and therefore better appreciated.

No artist can be measured in isolation; Mackintosh rose and flourished, as did his native city of Glasgow, when the fantasy of Art Nouveau was at its height. His artistic dreams were shared by countless others both on the Continent and in America — Horta, Gaudi, Hoffmann, Guimard, Klimt, Tiffany, Wright — all young men and all, like Mackintosh, trying to escape the vulgar excesses and the drab drudgery of the Victorian Industrial Revolution. Escape was a common artistic denominator: symbolism an issue of no little importance. Design, far from being an invisible act of industry, became a visible expression of both

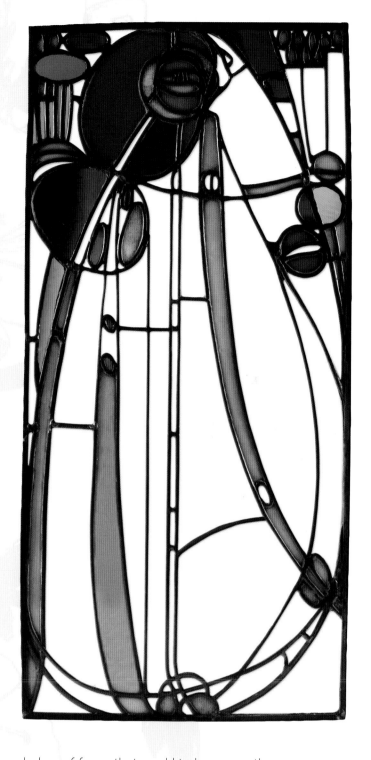

nationalism and culture. All were seeking a new vocabulary of forms that would truly express the spirit of the age. Mackintosh set himself the 'task of clothing in grace and beauty the new forms and conditions that modern developments of life ... insist upon'. Another Art Nouveau obsession was the search for *gesamtkunstwerk*, the total work of art. It was when he was working freely, for himself or for an enlightened patron such as Walter Blackie of The Hill House, that Mackintosh came nearest to achieving the concept.

Although there were personal circumstances, depression, decline and a tendency to drunkenness, Mackintosh's professional downfall was very much a shared experience. Factors affecting his practice were neither peculiar nor restricted. Many of his contemporaries were hit by a similar failure to procure architectural commissions. Some, like Mackintosh and Voysey, succumbed; others like Lutyens, Hoffman and Frank Lloyd Wright were able to ride out the storm. Very few continued to stamp a personal mark on the ensuing era. In Mackintosh's case there was a change of style: Derngate, in Northampton, vividly represented a new and modern approach more in accord with the jazz age. Unfortunately, although it featured in *Ideal Home* magazine, Mackintosh's name was not attached and so an important contribution to the modern era of architecture and interior design

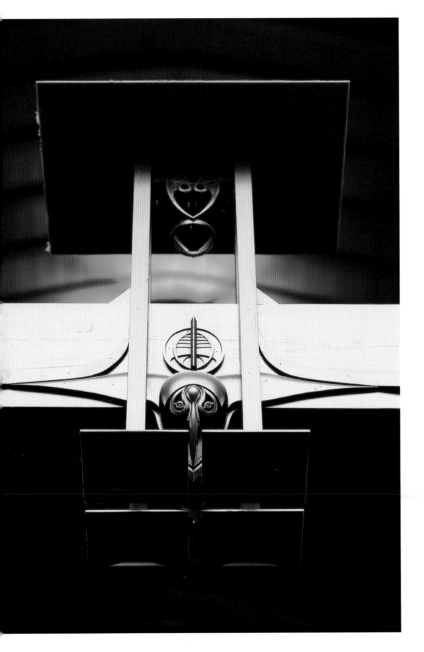

went unrecogniZed. In addition, by a savage quirk of fate, he was deprived of his main champions. Gleeson White, the editor of *The Studio* magazine who had heralded Mackintosh as the leader of a new style, died. Muthesius, author of *The English House*, who had introduced his work to a German and Austrian public, was on the wrong side of the First World War. And Miss Cranston, the redoubtable doyenne of the Glasgow Tea Room movement, sold off her tea rooms and retired on the death of her husband.

Of course, as this book ably demonstrates, Mackintosh was more than just an architect and interior designer. His furniture, light fittings and cutlery designs are still being manufactured. The fact that they continue to have a separate existence from the very specific location for which they were designed in some way

demonstrates the skill and artistry of the man. His work as a textile designer and watercolour artist, a rather neglected and therefore lesser known area of his artistic oeuvre, is also evaluated. The real impact of Mackintosh's work and life must be measured in the context of the early twentieth-century history of art, architecture and design. It is an important and still viable contribution, and his lasting popularity demonstrates how what seemed to have been a life of failure has left a lasting legacy of international significance.

ANNE ELLIS

INTRODUCTION

Genius, innovator, visionary, perfectionist, forerunner of Modernism and precursor to Art Deco, Charles Rennie Mackintosh has become synonymous with any number of labels. The inevitable habit of categorizing is never more poignant than when applied to Mackintosh, and yet he is by the very nature of his work indefinable. His unique expression and the language of his artistic energy set him apart from his contemporaries and those that followed, while providing a bridge spanning the chasm from Victoriana to the new century.

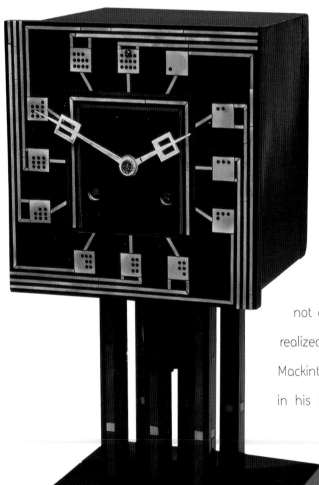

'Old forms in new ways' was Mackintosh's premise as he grappled with the diversity of translating the traditional into a modern context. Mackintosh's vision was for a new language of expression, a new way forward for architecture and designing and one that would be led by the Scottish. He sought to influence those around him, to redefine their artistic goals, and yet he never became the 'leader' or figurehead that he should have been in order to achieve a 'school' of design. He trod a solitary path and, so doing, was not able to see his vision for the future of architecture realized. It was a great tragedy that the fiercely nationalistic Mackintosh was never given the recognition that he deserved in his home town or country. Despite this, it was his intuitive perception of artistic endeavour that undoubtedly opened doors for those to follow. The Glasgow School of Art was visionary and inimitable in its conception; the dawn of the 'white room' and his simple, uncluttered approach to interior and exterior design was immediately at odds with the Victorian sensibilities of the time. Was it modern? Yes, within its context, although Mackintosh never sacrificed ornament or decorative detail to achieve his distinctive look. His modernity was inviolable, his expression unique, yet it was Peter Behrens who was credited with building the first 'modern' building when he designed New Ways for Mr Bassett-Lowke in 1925. Mackintosh was the ultimate master of synthesis: synthesis of form for function and of ornament with modernity. Part of Mackintosh's brilliance lay in his ability to meld the organic and the geometric seamlessly, the decorative and the functional, with neither at the aesthetic or utilitarian expense of the other.

That Mackintosh's life was beset with poor timing, bad luck and irony is a given. He died in poverty at a relatively young age, having lived the last years of his life abroad in isolation from his friends. But to view his life and works with a sense of melancholic sympathy is a mistake. The extraordinary intensity that Mackintosh devoted to his early architectural commissions, most especially the Glasgow School of Art, was never lost. He embraced each facet of his career with the same seriousness of intent. His textile and furniture designs and finally his watercolours were treated with equal artistic vision and enthusiasm. His decision to devote himself to watercolour painting was

perhaps not so surprising in the light of his lifelong affinity with nature and sketching. The work that he produced, however, was astonishing and it is rarely afforded the critical acclaim that it deserves. Although his architecture had voiced an undeniably new language, his painting style was virtually unique. The difference being that the evolution of his architectural voice, though not derivative, is certainly traceable through different areas of influence, while his watercolour landscapes are singularly modern in expression.

What of the man behind the great name? 'Tosh' to his friends, or 'Uncle Toshie' to his younger admirers, was as flamboyant and complex as his formidable talent would suggest. As a student, he enjoyed the wild, hedonistic days of the art school. He immersed himself in the progressive artistic culture synonymous with the school under the direction of Francis Newbery, a man who would be a lifelong friend, patron and supporter to Mackintosh. The 'Glasgow Four', consisting of Mackintosh and his friend Herbert MacNair and the Macdonald sisters, Margaret and Frances, forged a name for

themselves based on their similar artistic expression. Their studios became meeting points for long nights of discussions and parties, swapped ideologies and shared artistic aims. Mackintosh was pivotal to the group, admired for his talent and extrovert personality amongst the students. Attractive, warm-hearted, generous and proud, but also prone to violent tempers, arrogance and inflexibility, he was a complex individual, irascible and with a legendary attention to every minuscule detail. Undoubtedly, aspects of his character were significant in the crumbling of his architectural career. Accounts indicate he was difficult to work for and with – his working methods were fluid and

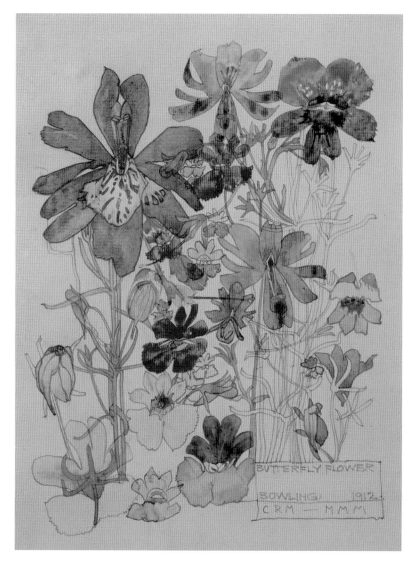

creative, and his architectural plans a point of departure for him rather than a concrete projection of design. Frustrated by lack of recognition and the inability to change the ideas of those around him, he suffered increasingly from depression and loss of self-confidence, resulting in his first move away from Glasgow, to Walberswick, in an attempt to heal old wounds.

The one constant in Mackintosh's life was an extraordinary woman without whom one must wonder what might have befallen him. Margaret Macdonald was four years older than Charles and won his heart in the late 1890s when he was still engaged to Jessie Keppie, sister to John Keppie, Mackintosh's business partner. By 1900, Charles had broken Jessie's heart and married Margaret, sealing a relationship of immense stability and mutual respect. Margaret provided the even keel to Charles's temperament. The couple were popular amongst their circle and on their move to London they immersed themselves in the local culture, throwing spectacular parties and becoming involved in theatre and arts groups. The intensity of their symbiotic relationship was never diluted by children – they never had children of their own, although they were both extremely fond of them and Margaret would often throw elaborate children's parties for their friends' youngsters. Margaret was a member of the Four and was a highly talented artist and craftswoman, working in a similar style to her sister Frances and Herbert MacNair. Margaret's influence on Charles is often scathingly referred to. Her work was distinctively mystical and ethereal, often associated with the Symbolist and Aesthetic

movements, and was of a romantically decorative nature. She is held responsible by some for holding Charles back artistically, the conjecture being that he would have gone on to a greater degree of Modernism without her influence. The more decorative aspects of his work are cited as being reflective of Margaret's hand and as being detrimental to his work as an architect and designer. To believe this is to misinterpret Mackintosh completely. The decorative element to his style was of great importance to Mackintosh, inextricable from his architecture and treatment of form. His work was far deeper than simple ornament and manipulation of space – every aspect of his designs had some meaning or significance to him. Invariably, the sheer wonder at his work and its unique decorative aesthetic overshadows the significance of every detail that he created. In a relationship as close as that of Charles and Margaret, both personal and working, it is inevitable that they shared inspiration and ideas. Charles referred to Margaret as a 'genius' in the face of his mere 'talent'. She was his rock and stalwart, steadfastly guiding them both through periods of extreme difficulty. The Mackintosh style is surely a collaboration, an artistic joining and flowering from a relationship of mutual artistic respect and talent.

Mackintosh's greatest architectural work came at the beginning of his career, seen in the domestic commission for The Hill House (1902) and, of course, the Glasgow School of Art (1896–99 and 1907–09). His productive working career was incredibly short, and by the time the Glasgow School of Art was completed his fortunes were already on the decline. It is the greatest irony that the triumph of his career also signalled its demise. Mackintosh's vision for a new way forward was misunderstood and largely ignored by his countrymen and it was on the Continent that he finally achieved some measure of distinction. Mackintosh's work and that of the Four was widely acclaimed by their contemporaries in Vienna, whose own artistic language had developed along similar routes to that of the young Scots. Mackintosh did not execute a vast number of commissions abroad despite his popularity, probably due to his large workload at that time in Glasgow. By the time he would have been in a position to work extensively abroad, the First World War had begun and his close relationship with the Continent was effectively severed.

On his death, his estate was valued at a paltry £88, four chairs being valued at £1, and yet he is now regarded as one of the greatest designers of modern times. Some years ago, one of his writing desks sold for the princely sum of £720,000 and his furniture is widely sought after and collected. His death passed virtually unnoticed in 1928 and, by a typically twisted hand of fate, the following year a group of Austrian architects wrote to invite Mackintosh to Vienna, to honour his prodigious influence on the evolution of their architecture and design. Unrecognized during his lifetime and forgotten for years, the spirit of Mackintosh has at last been rekindled. Finally, the true measure of his genius is starting to be understood, the mystery of his artistic evolution detangled and his unique artistic language comprehended.

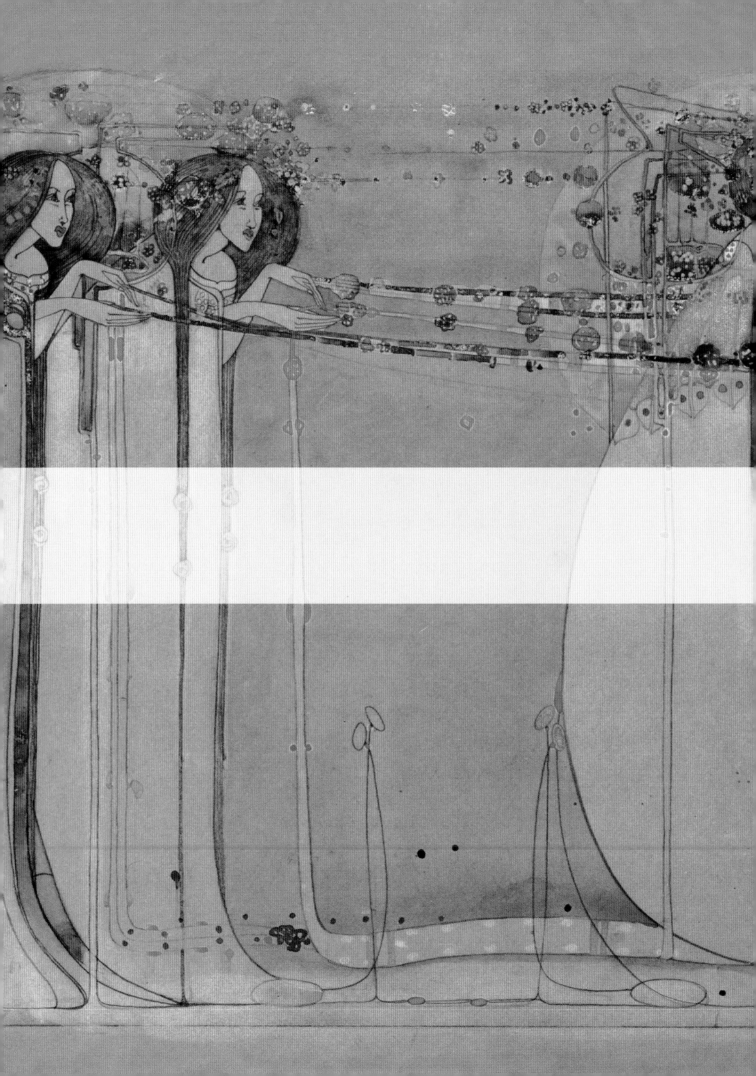

LIFE

DOMINO CLOCK, 1917

© Art Gallery & Museum, Kelvingrove, Glasgow, Scotland, Glasgow City Council
(Museums)/The Bridgeman Art Library

CREATED
Derngate,
Northampton

MEDIUM
Ebonized wood
with ivory and
plastic inlay

**SERIES/PERIOD/
MOVEMENT**
Derngate designs

Number 78 Derngate was the most significant of Mackintosh's sparse commissions at this time, along with the decoration for the Dug Out, in the basement of the Willow Tea Rooms. The Dug Out project was again to include all interior design, furniture, fixtures and fittings, and demonstrates Mackintosh's inexhaustible supply of innovative ideas. He used strong geometric forms that appear modern and Oriental in conception. The Willow Tea Rooms were the only tea rooms for which Mackintosh designed the exterior façade. This gave the rooms a continuation in handling and vision from the exterior to the interior, something that Mackintosh was greatly concerned with. The Domino Clock was designed for Bassett-Lowke in 1917 for the Derngate residence. The bold linear form and use of ebonized wood were typical of Mackintosh's designs at this time. The clock fitted perfectly within the scheme of the house, which was based around patterns of chequerboards, lines and triangles. Dominoes was a popular game at this time and the domino motif was one that Mackintosh often employed.

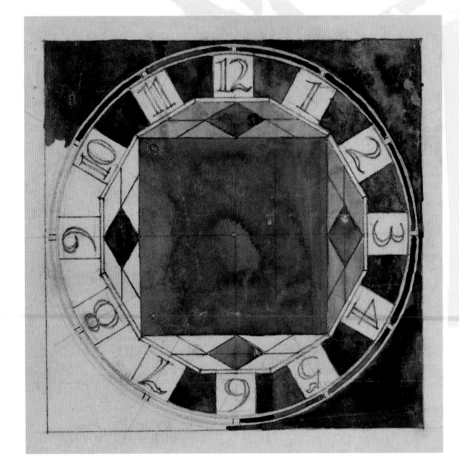

DESIGN FOR A CLOCK FACE FOR W. J. BASSETT-LOWKE, 1917

© Christie's Images Ltd
When it was eventually finished, the green detail on this clock face was fashioned from erinoid. This was an early form of plastic which Mackintosh began to use on his furniture, mostly for decorative inlays, around 1917.

CABINET MADE FOR 14 KINGSBOROUGH GARDENS, GLASGOW, 1902

© The Fine Art Society, London, UK/The Bridgeman Art Library

The early years of the 1900s were a period of intense activity for Mackintosh. He had several commissions at Kilmacolm, one for the Gate Lodge at Auchenbothie and another for a house in the area, details of which are now lost. He designed the House at Bridge of Weir for Alfred Todd, delivered the lecture 'Seemliness' and his work was illustrated in *Dekorative Kunst* and *Deutsche Kunst und Dekoration*. Also in 1902 he was commissioned by Mrs Rowat to complete a series of interior decorations for the family home at 14 Kingsborough Gardens, Glasgow. Mrs Rowat was the mother of Francis Newbery's wife Jessie. Mackintosh was responsible for the wall decorations, in the form of stencilling, and for designing fireplaces, fixtures, fittings and some furniture. The cabinet pictured here is one of a matching pair. Seen with the doors open the piece is simple, yet beautiful and includes a stylized female figure holding a rosebud on the inside of each door. His use of silver leaf and fine coloured glass adds an opulent note to the piece that was crafted from painted Scottish oak.

CREATED
Glasgow

MEDIUM
Painted oak

**SERIES/PERIOD/
MOVEMENT**
Furniture design
of early 1900s

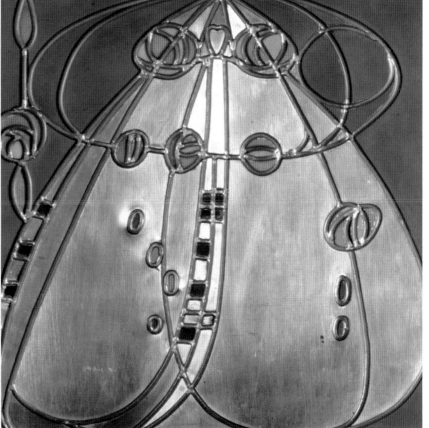

DETAIL FROM AN EBONIZED MAHOGANY WRITING CABINET, 1904

© Christie's Images Ltd
Both the cabinet (main picture) and the detail pictured here feature one of Mackintosh's motifs: the stylized rose. The combination of organic flowing lines with geometric shapes is key to his style.

DINING ROOM SUITE, C. 1918–19

© The Fine Art Society, London, UK/The Bridgeman Art Library

CREATED
London

MEDIUM
Wood, inlaid with
mother-of-pearl and
aluminium

**SERIES/PERIOD/
MOVEMENT**
London furniture
designs

Bassett-Lowke continued to provide Mackintosh with small commissions after the major redecoration of Derngate, 1916–17, and in 1919 he was commissioned to redesign the Derngate guest room. The guest room would become the most original of the decorative schemes throughout the house and was startlingly modern in concept. The room has since been recreated as part of the Mackintosh House at the Hunterian Gallery in Glasgow. The twin beds in the room demonstrate Mackintosh's use of the square motif as his only decorative feature. This was something he employed frequently during this period, often using inlaid squares of mother-of-pearl, as seen in this dining room table and chairs. This dining room set that was commissioned by Harry Franklin, director of a prominent engineering firm, is sturdy and utilitarian in design. In 1919–20, Mackintosh worked on a studio cottage and pigeon house for the acclaimed photographer E. O. Hoppé (1878–1972), who was also involved with the activities of the Plough group. The studio cottage, which was created from the shell of an old gamekeeper's house at the Little Hedgecourt estate in East Grinstead, Sussex, is not regarded as a particularly memorable piece of Mackintosh's work.

TABLE WITH MOTHER-OF-PEARL INLAY, 1918
© The Fine Art Society, London, UK/The Bridgeman Art Library
The pieces here reflect Mackintosh's interest in Japanese design. He was impressed by its restraint and emphasis on natural materials and simple forms, and tried to echo this in his own design.

CONVERSAZIONE PROGRAMME, DESIGNED FOR THE GLASGOW ARCHITECTURAL ASSOCIATION, 1894

© Christie's Images Ltd

CREATED
Glasgow

MEDIUM
Lithograph in
black and green
on blue paper

**SERIES/PERIOD/
MOVEMENT**
Poster designs
of the 1890s

In 1885, Francis Newbery (1855–1946), an Englishman, had been appointed head of the Glasgow School of Art. He inaugurated himself within the Scottish culture making few waves and was readily accepted. He quickly recognized Mackintosh's talent and modernity and introduced him and MacNair to Margaret and Frances Macdonald. The Macdonald sisters were also students at the school and were developing a style along similar lines to Mackintosh and MacNair. The four quickly formed a close friendship and began to work together, becoming known as the 'Glasgow Four'. They exhibited together and their unique vision became the foundation for the emergence of the Glasgow style. In 1893, Mackintosh delivered a lecture urging his fellow architects to 'go straight to Nature', to 'clothe modern ideas with modern dress', a suggestion contrary to the conservative view of many

GLASGOW SCHOOL OF ART: VIEW OF A STUDIO

© Glasgow School of Art, Scotland/
The Bridgeman Art Library
An artist himself, Mackintosh knew
what would be required from this
hard-working building; one aspect
of this to which he paid particular
attention was the provision of good
lighting, both natural and artificial.

THE CUA[...]

CHAS. R. MACKINTOSH

academics. The Glasgow Four built their style around fluid organic shapes, sinewy tendrils and stylized forms of leaves, trees, branches and stalks. Their figures were as lean and willowy as the foliage they depicted. *The Conversazione Programme* is typical of this period in Mackintosh's work and combines the boldness of architectural line with a curvilinear sweep of organic form.

MACKINTOSH

GLASGOW SCHOOL OF ART: VIEW OF THE EXTERIOR, BUILT 1897–99

© Glasgow School of Art, Scotland/The Bridgeman Art Library

CREATED
Glasgow

MEDIUM
Architecture

SERIES/PERIOD/ MOVEMENT
Glasgow School of Art

In 1896, the Glasgow Four were invited to exhibit at the Arts and Crafts Society Exhibition in London. They failed to get the recognition that they deserved, but their work was spotted by Gleeson White of *The Studio* magazine. He would go on to feature the artists' work frequently in the respected art journal and was significant in publicizing the work of the Four across England and the Continent. The same year, a competition was announced to draw up designs for a new building to house the Glasgow School of Art. Eleven firms entered and Honeyman and Keppie won with Mackintosh's plans. There was an immediate outcry. The strong friendship between Mackintosh and Francis Newbery, head of the school, was no secret and it was rumoured that that was why Mackintosh had secured the commission. Mackintosh's plans were also criticized for being Art Nouveau in style and for failing to register the importance of historic traditions of architecture. His plans were, in fact, an extraordinary accomplishment for a young architect and addressed the difficult site parameters head-on and creatively.

GLASGOW SCHOOL OF ART: DIRECTOR'S ROOM, 1897–99

© Glasgow School of Art, Scotland/The Bridgeman Art Library
Mackintosh's interiors were underpinned by the Modernist ethos that believed buildings and objects should reflect the needs of the user, rather than be adorned with unnecessary ostentatious ornamentation.

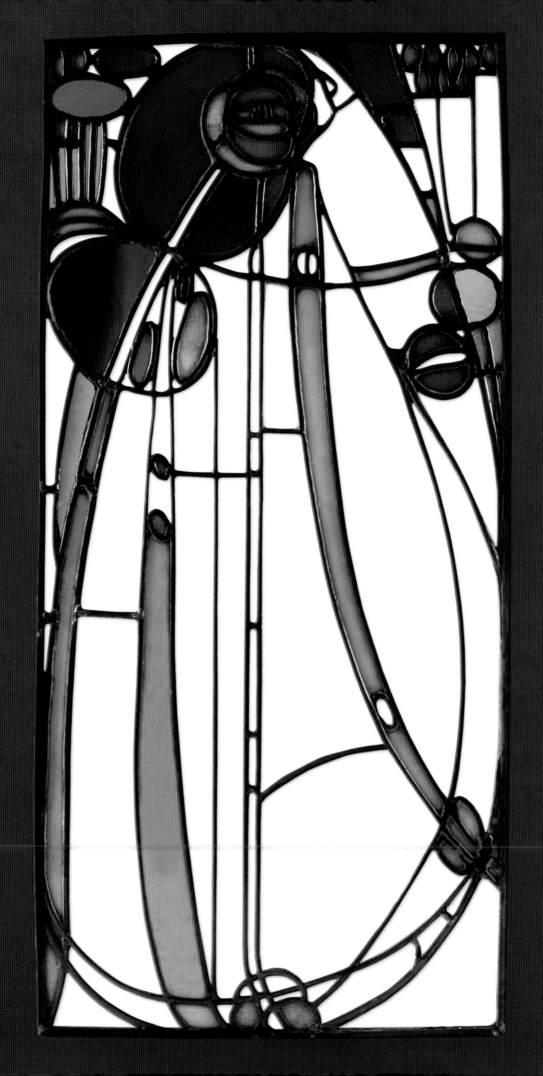

GLASS PANEL, 1902

© Hunterian Museum & Art Gallery, University of Glasgow

The Mackintoshes had been warmly received on the Continent following their inclusion at the Eighth Secessionist Exhibition in Vienna, 1900. In 1902, they were commissioned by Fritz Wärndorfer to design a music salon for his house. The finished room was held in high regard by many critics and was considered a masterpiece of unity. Sadly the room was later destroyed and nothing of it remains. The same year saw the International Exhibition of Modern Decorative Art in Turin, for which Mackintosh designed a series of three rooms. The most notable of these was the Rose Boudoir, panelled in white-painted woodwork and furnished with his high-backed chairs; the room was the result of both Charles and Margaret's artistic input. A characteristic of Mackintosh's style was the use of coloured glass and glass panels to highlight and enhance a visual plane, be it architectural or in furniture. Panels such as the one pictured, and another one of a stylized female form done in the same year, would be effective in filtering rich and varied light into a room.

CREATED
Glasgow

MEDIUM
Stained glass

SERIES/PERIOD/
MOVEMENT
Glass panels

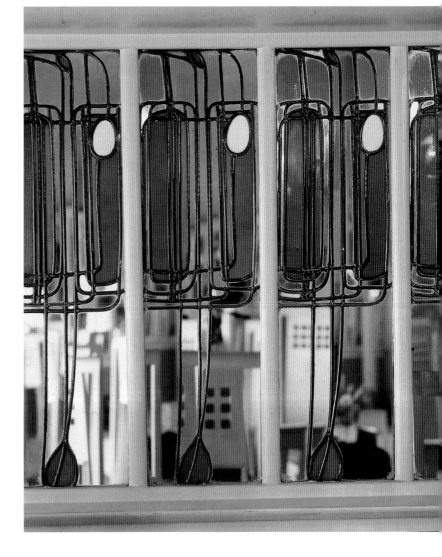

GLASS PANEL FROM THE WILLOW TEA ROOMS, 1903

© Anthony Oliver

Despite Mackintosh often being labelled as the pioneer of Modernism, he veered from the utilitarianism of the movement. He believed that people should live in a work of art, a belief echoed in the beauty of this panel.

DETAIL FROM AN EBONIZED MAHOGANY WRITING CABINET, 1904

© Christie's Images Ltd

CREATED
Glasgow

MEDIUM
Stained glass

SERIES/PERIOD/ MOVEMENT
Furniture design of early 1900s

Mackintosh was introduced to Walter Blackie in 1902 when the publishing magnate had bought a plot of land to the north of Helensburgh, not far from Glasgow. After showing Blackie the Windyhill House, built in 1902 for William Davidson Junior, Mackintosh was commissioned to design The Hill House. The Hill House is widely regarded as the best example of Mackintosh's domestic architecture. During 1902 and 1903, Mackintosh created the interiors for the Moscow Exhibition of Modern Architecture and Design, further enhancing his growing reputation abroad. In 1903, his designs for Liverpool Cathedral were published and in the same year he returned to work for Catherine Cranston, embarking on the Willow Tea Rooms. Mackintosh worked on the interiors and furniture designs for The Hill House during 1904. He designed three similar writing desks, one of which he used himself. These cabinets were crafted from expensive materials: ebonized wood, mother-of-pearl and pear-wood inlays, and ivory and exotic stained-glass features. The interiors of the desks were as beautiful as the exteriors, with pigeon-hole divisions and a sliding writing surface.

THE MAY QUEEN, 1900

MARGARET MACDONALD MACKINTOSH BORN 1864 Tipton, Wolverhampton **DIED** 1933

© Christie's Images Ltd

The echo of line and shape can be seen across the work of Mackintosh and his wife Margaret Macdonald Mackintosh. Their symbiotic relationship nourished their art, though many argue that Margaret's influence changed Charles's artistic direction.

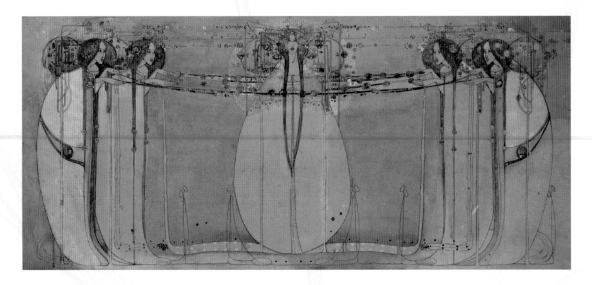

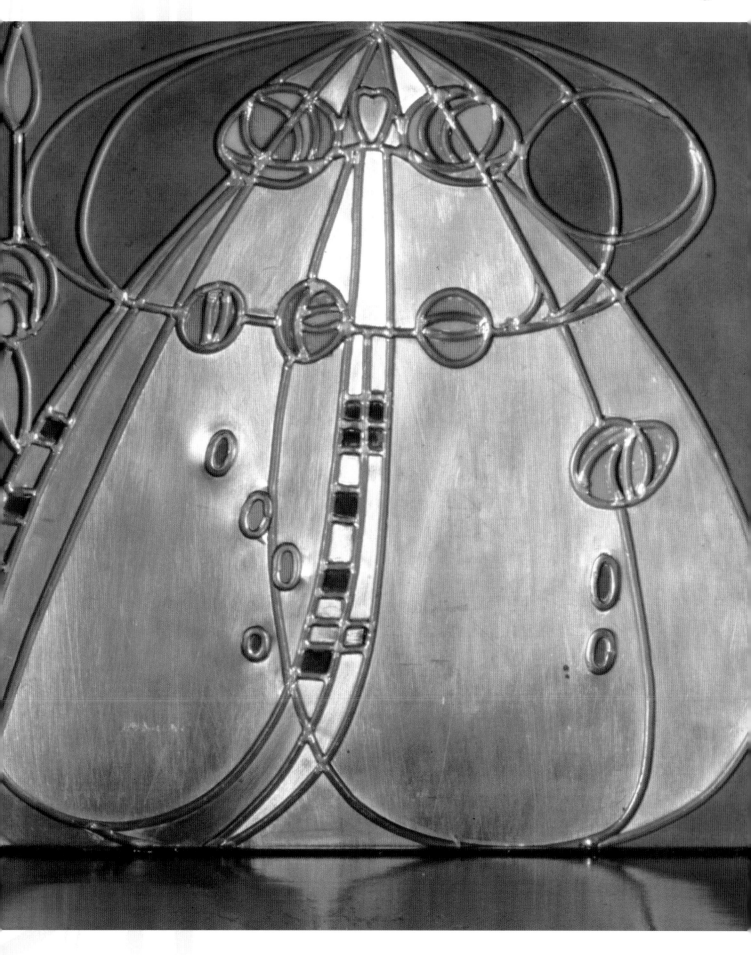

GLASGOW SCHOOL OF ART: DIRECTOR'S ROOM, 1897–99

© Glasgow School of Art, Scotland/The Bridgeman Art Library

CREATED
Glasgow

MEDIUM
Interior design

SERIES/PERIOD/ MOVEMENT
Glasgow School of Art

The Glasgow School of Art was built in two stages separated by a number of years. The initial stage, which was budgeted at £14,000, was completed by 1899, but had run over the costing by more than a third. The school in its final state stands as the summation of Mackintosh's design articulation and is a singularly brilliant synthesis of function through form. Mackintosh's concern with detail, down to the smallest element, provided the school with a completely unified artistic statement, from the interior to the exterior and all the fittings and furnishings in between. The Director's Room is a classic example of Mackintosh's use of simple form made dramatic through light and carefully placed decoration. The room is at first austere, but the light from the deep arched window recess reflects from the white panelling to bathe the entire room. This is one of the first examples of Mackintosh's 'white rooms', something he would return to in later interiors. The clean, simple lines of the room call to mind the traditional stone interior walls of Scottish castles.

EXTERIOR OF WINDYHILL, KILMACOLM, 1901

© Anthony Oliver

Both the house and the room pictured here reflect Mackintosh's take on the Scottish vernacular. This was a key part of his style, as were the fluid lines and geometric shapes employed in much of his work.

TABLE WITH MOTHER-OF-PEARL INLAY, 1918

© The Fine Art Society, London, UK/The Bridgeman Art Library

CREATED
London

MEDIUM
Stained mahogany
wood with mother-
of-pearl inlay

**SERIES/PERIOD/
MOVEMENT**
London furniture
designs

The London Salon of the Independents was instigated to give any artist the opportunity to exhibit. A small annual membership fee was charged because, unlike the Salon des Indépendants in Paris, the London group was not supported by the government. This put them at a huge disadvantage and the members struggled to keep the group going. Mackintosh was involved in trying to establish exhibition space for the society to get it up and running. Sadly, nowhere was found and the group was eventually disseminated. At around the same time both Margaret and Charles became involved in the Plough, a performing arts group formed for 'the purpose of stimulating interest in good art of an unconventional kind'. The Plough's innovative approach to play production was based on involving the author/composer closely in the artistic presentation of their work and the performances became very popular.

Mackintosh had first turned towards rigid geometric shapes in his designs for the furniture at The Hill House, c. 1904. This pattern of design was then further realized in his work at Derngate, 1916–17. The use of simple mother-of-pearl inlay was an aesthetic device that Mackintosh used frequently during this period.

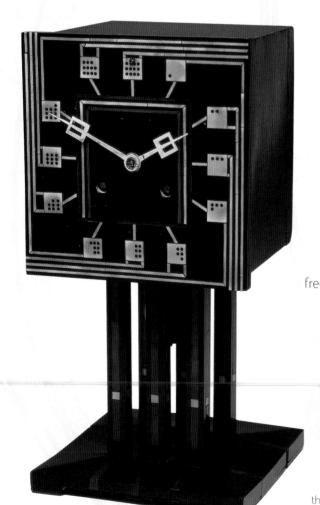

DOMINO CLOCK, 1917
© Art Gallery & Museum, Kelvingrove, Scotland,
Glasgow City Council (Museums)/ The Bridgeman Art Library
The geometric patterns applied to these domestic objects
are in keeping with the advances that were taking place in
the Modernist movement at the time, which also favoured
the use of a monochrome palette.

WASHSTAND, C. 1917

© The Fine Art Society, London, UK/The Bridgeman Art Library

Since their move to London, the Mackintoshes had established themselves within a tight-knit circle of artists and artisans. Thomas Howarth, in his substantial reflection on the Mackintoshes' life, refers to Margaret as an enthusiastic party thrower, especially children's parties even though the Mackintoshes had no children of their own. Her parties were planned and co-ordinated down to the last detail, a method not dissimilar to the design treatment of their interiors. Charles and Margaret were flamboyantly unconventional; Charles in his long academic-style cloak and Margaret in dresses that she designed and made herself. They became great friends with Margaret Morris, an accomplished dance teacher who had opened a studio in Chelsea the year before the Mackintoshes arrived in London. Margaret Morris's studio became a centre of performing arts and creative thinking, an atmosphere that the Mackintoshes were naturally attracted to. During this period, Mackintosh worked on textile and furniture designs, producing pieces that truly foresaw the emergence of Modernism. The washstand, pictured, demonstrates his use of inlaid mother-of-pearl in simple squares, distinctly different from his earlier Glasgow style of curvilinear forms.

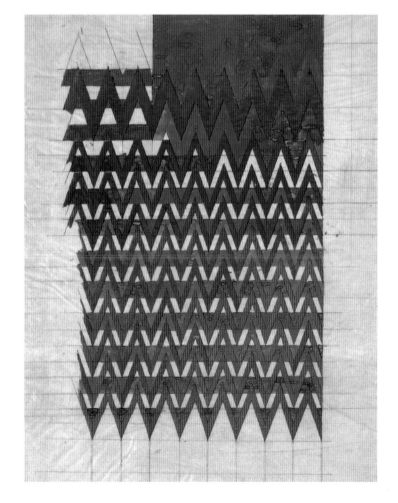

CREATED
London

MEDIUM
Mahogany, inlaid with mother-of-pearl and green erinoid, with glass backplate

SERIES/PERIOD/MOVEMENT
London furniture designs

FABRIC DESIGN, 1916

© Christie's Images Ltd
One of the secrets of Mackintosh's skill as a designer was that he could adapt his trademark use of shape and form to so many different objects, as here with the washstand and fabric design.

SOCIETY

SIGN FOR THE WILLOW TEA ROOMS

© Anthony Oliver

CREATED
Glasgow

MEDIUM
Iron

**SERIES/PERIOD/
MOVEMENT**
Tea room designs

The Willow Tea Rooms were built on Sauchiehall Street, a popular and fashionable area of Glasgow. 'Sauchiehall', translating to 'alley of the willows', provided the foundation for the entire decorative scheme throughout which Mackintosh alluded to and evoked the willow tree. Although he was able to design the façade and interior arrangement of the building, he had to work with an existing structure situated on a narrow and restrictive site. His solution to the scheme was a brilliant display of startling Modernism, far ahead of its time. He created a building that rests easily between its neighbours and yet also stands alone in its harmonious asymmetry. One of the most striking features of the exterior was the first-floor expanse of glittering window spanning over six metres (18 feet). This marked on the exterior the jewel-like room of the Salon De Luxe on the interior. The façade was white and divided by a narrow projecting hood, below which the first-floor window sat in a gently curving plane. Above, the façade curves on one side and is punctured by recessed grid-like windows. The black-and-white chequerboard design on the sign is continued through the façade, running up each side of the building and decorating the window surrounds.

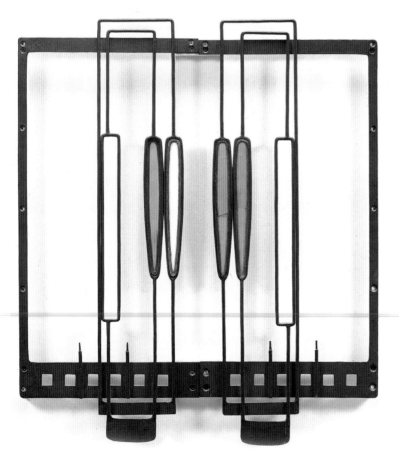

RAILING FROM THE WILLOW TEA ROOMS, GLASGOW, C. 1901–04

© Christie's Images Ltd

Glasgow's tea rooms emerged out of the burgeoning temperance movement at the turn of the twentieth century. They served all classes of society with non-alcoholic refreshments at a moderate price in elegant surroundings.

INTERIOR OF THE STAIR TOWER OF
SCOTLAND STREET SCHOOL, 1904

© Anthony Oliver

D ue mostly to the financial restraints of the commission, the Scotland Street School was supremely simple in design with ornamentation occurring only around the doors and windows. The required segregation of the co-educational system resulted in a design of symmetrical form, with separate entrances for the girls and boys, as well as separate stairways, cloakrooms, classrooms and playgrounds. Through the simplicity of the design, however, shines the brilliance of aesthetic realization. The soaring verticality of the stair towers lends a quasi-religious solemnity to the structure, enhanced by the bank of rhythmic vertical windows that anticipate Modernism. As is typical of Mackintosh's designs, the interior space is of equal or greater importance than the exterior. Every detail, even down to the arrangement of the staircase with its metal banisters echoing the verticality of the windows, was considered and executed with a brilliant synthesis of form. The detail, pictured, demonstrates Mackintosh's use of small insets of coloured glass and his geometric pattern of triangles and squares. Both of these were motifs that he would come back to again and again through his designs.

CREATED
Glasgow

MEDIUM
Stained glass

**SERIES/PERIOD/
MOVEMENT**
School designs

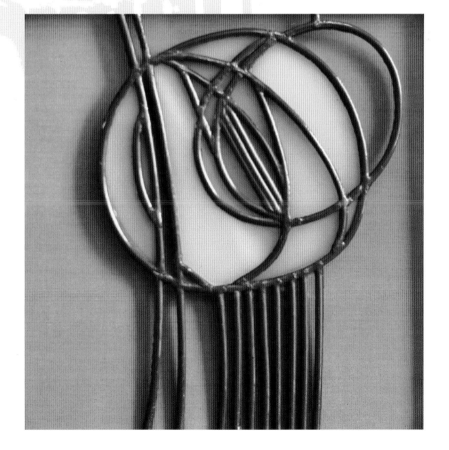

ROSE MOTIF, THE HILL HOUSE,
HELENSBURGH, C. 1902–03

© Anthony Oliver
Mackintosh's fascination with Oriental art was apparent through his use of motifs. Decorative motifs have a special meaning in Oriental art, frequently being used to teach essential lessons in life.

THE WHITE COCKADE: ILLUSTRATION FOR A MENU, 1911

© Christie's Images Ltd

CREATED
Glasgow

MEDIUM
Lithographic print,
with overlaid paper

**SERIES/PERIOD/
MOVEMENT**
Tea room designs

**MARGARET
MACDONALD
MACKINTOSH**
BORN 1864 Tipton,
Wolverhampton
DIED 1933

King Edward died in 1910 and was succeeded by his son George V. He was greeted by a political maelstrom begun in 1909 with 'the people's budget', instigated by the Liberal Welshman Lloyd George. The Lords were bitterly opposed to the increased taxes and the ensuing rivalry peaked in 1911 with the 'Parliament Bill'. This effectively removed power from the Lords resulting in the Commons becoming virtually the sole legislative body. The same year saw the first Post-Impressionist exhibition in London, described by the harshest critics as 'the negation of civilization'. This was also the year of another Glasgow International Exhibition, as the city continued to demonstrate its success. Miss Cranston opened a restaurant, The White Cockade, at the exhibition and commissioned the Mackintoshes to design the layout and furnishings. Margaret and Charles often collaborated on the tea-room designs, although in this instance the menu card for The White Cockade is attributed to Margaret herself. At the same time, the Mackintoshes were also working on designs for the Cloister Room and the Chinese Room at Miss Cranston's Ingram Street Tea Rooms.

DESIGNS FOR WRITING DESKS FOR THE INGRAM STREET TEA ROOMS, 1909

© Christie's Images Ltd
In 1900, Mackintosh had the chance to redesign a whole room at the Ingram Street Tea Rooms.
He worked with the owner, Miss Cranston, on all of her four Glasgow tea rooms.

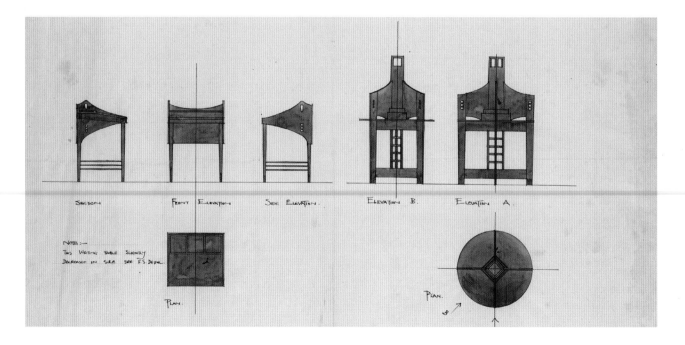

THE·PRINCIPAL·SUPPLIES·USED·IN
MISS·CRANSTONS:
EXHIBITION·CAFES:
·· ARE·FROM·THE·FOLLOWING

·· WELL·KNOWN·SOURCES ·

TEA·† COFFEE·	AND·MELROSE+Co 39·GEORGE·ST EDINBURGH
BREAD	WM·BEATTIE DENNISTON· BAKERY GLASGOW·
CAKES·	MISS·CRANSTONS BAKERY· 292·ST·VINCENT·ST GLASGOW·
BISCUITS·	McFARLANE· LANG+Co· VICTORIA·WORKS· GLASGOW·
FISH·† POULTRY	THOS·ANDERSON 58·60·WEST·NILE·ST· GLASGOW·
COLD MEAT· SPECIALTIES·	R·D·WADDELL· NAPIERSHALL·ST· GLASGOW·
MILK·† CREAM	HUGH·HAMILTON HIGH·JOHN·ST· GLASGOW·
CHOCOLATES·	CAILLERS· BROC· SWITZERLAND·

THE WHITE COCKADE

RARE LADDER-BACK CHAIR FOR THE WILLOW TEA ROOMS, 1903

© Christie's Images Ltd

Miss Cranston's tea rooms enjoyed their great success based in part on the variety of facilities that they offered. In true entrepreneurial spirit, she used the 'tea room' as her point of departure and added to it: billiard rooms, ladies' rooms, smoking rooms and restaurants. Her tea rooms provided every available source for relaxation and spending money and catered to a wide section of society. She was herself known as a singularly unusual and striking woman and these qualities she sought to utilize in her tea rooms. Mackintosh, as one of the most innovative designers of his time, was the ideal champion of her cause. For the Willow Tea Rooms he created three separate areas, without the use of partitioning walls: a front saloon decorated mostly in white; the rear saloon, which was much darker; and the gallery from which an open stair led to the ground floor. The ladder-back chair design was intended to symbolize the willow tree. On first glance the multiple chair backs in the dining room (rear saloon) would appear as a forest of willows. This heavy, darker furniture was in direct contrast to the white-painted high-backed chairs in the Salon De Luxe.

CREATED
Glasgow

MEDIUM
Ebonized oak

SERIES/PERIOD/MOVEMENT
Tea room designs

SETTLE FROM THE DUG OUT, MISS CRANSTON'S WILLOW TEA ROOMS

© The Fine Art Society, London, UK/The Bridgeman Art Library
The Willow Tea Rooms were situated on Sauchiehall Street, which in Gaelic means
'alley of the willows'. Mackintosh echoed the theme of willow trees throughout the building's design.

DETAIL OF PRELIMINARY DESIGN FOR A MURAL DECORATION AT MISS CRANSTON'S BUCHANAN STREET TEA ROOMS, 1896–97

© Glasgow University Art Gallery, Scotland/The Bridgeman Art Library

CREATED
Glasgow

MEDIUM
Pencil and watercolour on tracing paper

SERIES/PERIOD/ MOVEMENT
Tea room designs

The economic boom of Glasgow based on shipping and heavy industries had a profound effect on the city, promoting great growth and expansion, but also creating severe social problems. Quite apart from the overcrowding of the working classes and related issues, there was a massive increase in alcoholism, leading to petty crimes and disorderly behaviour. The initial rise of the tea room in the late 1870s played a major part in combating this. They offered cheap, sociable places for people to congregate and pass the time. The splendid tea rooms typified by those of Miss Cranston evolved from the first humble tea shops.

Mackintosh worked on the Buchanan Street Tea Rooms with George Walton, an accomplished, though underrated designer who has never quite received the accolade he deserves. Walton undertook the majority of the commission, with Mackintosh being primarily responsible for the wall decorations. The design here formed a highly stylized frieze that ran around the walls of the general tea room on the first floor. Mackintosh's decorative scheme impressed Gleeson White, editor of *The Studio* magazine, who described it as 'an honest attempt at novelty'.

THE WHITE COCKADE: ILLUSTRATION FOR A MENU, 1911
MARGARET MACDONALD MACKINTOSH
BORN 1864 Tipton, Wolverhampton
DIED 1933
© Christie's Images Ltd
It is not known exactly how many of her husband's works Margaret Macdonald Mackintosh was involved with, but she is credited with being an important part of his more symbolic, figurative interior designs.

SETTLE FROM THE DUG OUT, MISS CRANSTON'S WILLOW TEA ROOMS

© The Fine Art Society, London, UK/The Bridgeman Art Library

Glasgow was famous for its tea rooms and Miss Cranston virtually single-handedly turned the concept of the humble tea room into something altogether larger, grander and more popular. The tea rooms evolved into much more than simple social gathering places, functioning as art galleries, exhibiting works by local artists the Glasgow Boys and epitomizing the upwardly mobile atmosphere generated through Glasgow's burgeoning industries. Inevitably, however, all good things come to an end and the staggering effects of the First World War saw the demise of the tea room. Miss Cranston struggled to keep her edge and opened the Dug Out in the basement of the Willow Tea Rooms during the war years. The Mackintoshes had by now settled in London, but Charles undertook the commission for the decorative scheme, producing designs for a memorial fireplace in a patriotic style, two canvases and some furniture, fixtures and fittings. The strongly geometric settle was typical of his later style, having moved away from the Art Nouveau-inspired forms seen in the Salon De Luxe. Miss Cranston sold the Willow Tea Rooms in 1919, two years after the death of her beloved husband.

CREATED
Glasgow

MEDIUM
Painted wood

SERIES/PERIOD/MOVEMENT
Tea room designs

ARMCHAIRS DESIGNED FOR THE BILLIARDS AND SMOKING ROOM AT MISS CRANSTON'S TEA ROOMS, 1898–99

© Christie's Images Ltd

Mackintosh made his interiors fit for purpose; the chairs pictured here are suitably baronial, appropriate for a male-only area. The settle was perfectly suited to a cutting-edge, arthouse café, just what the Dug Out was intended to be.

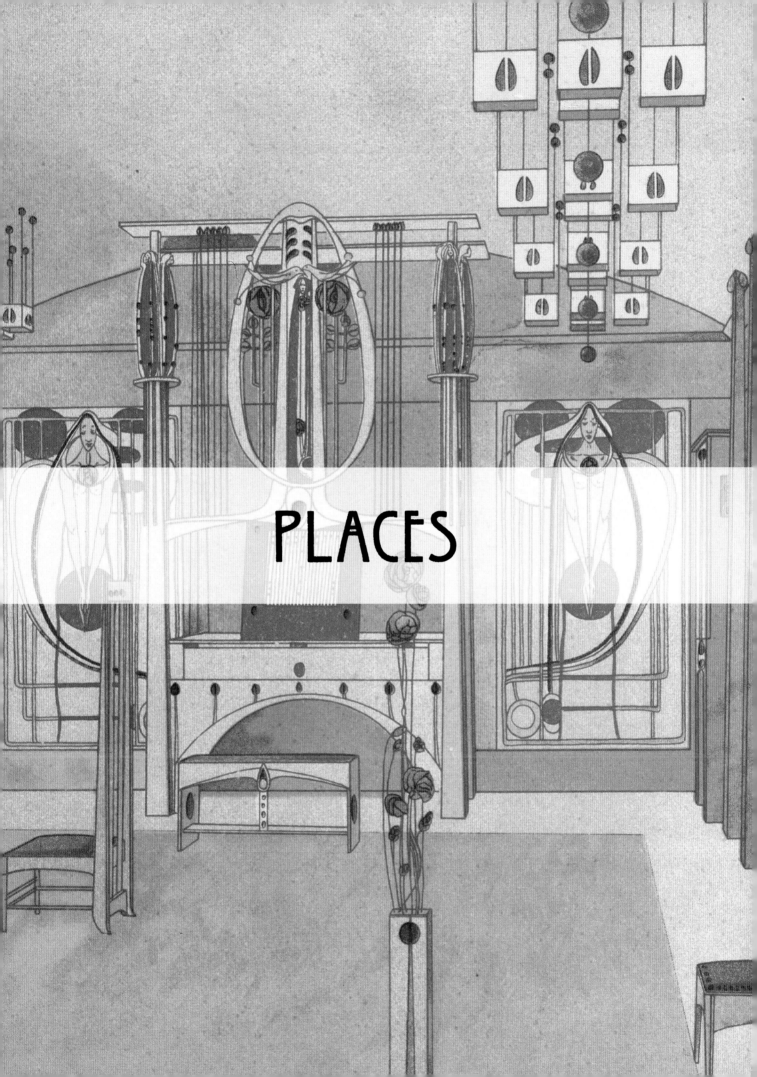

PLACES

THE ROAD THROUGH THE ROCKS, (DETAIL) C. 1926–27

CREATED
France

MEDIUM
Watercolour

**SERIES/PERIOD/
MOVEMENT**
Late period
landscapes

Mackintosh was especially drawn to the simple, squat forts that lined the French coast and the border with Spain. The great forms that rose out of the equally hulking rocks provided him with the design element and organic unity that he sought. Letters recall how Charles and Margaret would make trips out from their home at Port Vendres, often walking along the coastline with sketchbooks in hand. During their settlement in France, they also travelled to Italy and crossed the border to Spain where Mackintosh executed two paintings, *Fetges* and *A Spanish Farm*.

The forts dotted through their surrounding countryside became the subject of several watercolour studies. The slab-sided monumentality of man-made structures growing from the landscape and the contrast of the texture of rocks to fields to distant sea became a great source of inspiration to the artist. Charles worked slowly on his paintings, sometimes taking weeks to finish a single canvas, and preferred to work outside. It is interesting that, while Margaret and Charles often collaborated on projects through the years, there are no surviving paintings that indicate Margaret's involvement.

THE ROCKS, 1927

© The Fine Art Society, London, UK/
The Bridgeman Art Library
Mackintosh worked on his watercolours on sunny, windless mornings when the shadows were short and sharp. The finished pictures were often combinations of different views of the same place.

HOUSE FOR AN ART LOVER COMPETITION ENTRY:
DESIGN FOR A DINING ROOM, 1901

© The Stapleton Collection/The Bridgeman Art Library

PUBLISHED IN
Darmstadt

MEDIUM
Colour lithograph

**SERIES/PERIOD/
MOVEMENT**
House for an Art Lover

Mackintosh's design for the dining room is clean and simple. He devised wood panelling for the walls and a plain curved white ceiling with suspended decorative coloured-glass lights. Art Nouveau style insets at the top of each wood panel and the repeated use of stylized design motifs through the walls, carpet and furniture added to the encompassing air of unity through the room. Mackintosh's treatment of the interiors was in direct contrast to Baillie Scott. Baillie Scott had an

established reputation as one of the most

progressive artist-architects within the

Arts and Crafts movement in England and his work was

growing increasingly popular in Europe. In 1898. he had been

commissioned to furnish part of the new palace at Darmstadt

by the Grand Duke of Hesse, a project that greatly enhanced

his appeal on the Continent. Plans for his dining room show a

mass of unrelated decorative detail that competes with the

architectural schematics of the room. Nothing could have

been further from Mackintosh's quiet unified space.

HOUSE FOR AN ART LOVER COMPETITION ENTRY: DESIGN FOR A MUSIC ROOM WITH PANELS BY MARGARET MACDONALD MACKINTOSH, 1901

© The Stapleton Collection/The Bridgeman Art Library
The Mackintoshes worked on the designs for this house together, but because their entry was late, they were disqualified. Many still speculate on whether their design would have won had they not missed the deadline.

STUDY OF AN ENTRANCE PORCH, PALERMO CATHEDRAL, 1891

CREATED
Palermo

MEDIUM
Pencil and grey wash

**SERIES/PERIOD/
MOVEMENT**
Italian tour

As part of his tour Mackintosh travelled to the island of Sicily off the toe of Italy and visited the capital city, Palermo. Palermo was often referred to as the 'Garden City' based on the large number of beautifully designed public gardens that the city boasted. For Mackintosh, who had had a love of gardens since his childhood, Palermo must have been one of the most inspirational stops on his trip. Significantly, the National Exhibition of Palermo that ran from 1891 to 1892 would have afforded the young artist the opportunity to view the major artistic and architectural movements and cultural history of the area, within one frame. The city's cathedral was particularly riveting to Mackintosh who made several studies of it. He was fascinated by the intricate detail on the façade and the unusual combination of styles reflected through the building's long history. The cathedral dates back to the twelfth century and was originally built on the site of an Arab mosque. Much of the decorative detail that Mackintosh captured in his studies was inspired by the Islamic period, which is in contrast to the Norman apse.

GLASGOW SCHOOL OF ART: THE BOARDROOM, 1897–99

© Anthony Oliver

The lofty spaces of the Glasgow School of Art may have been in part inspired by Mackintosh's 1891 scholarship tour of Italy during which he sketched many of the great buildings of ancient classic architecture.

CATHEDRAL.
ENTRANCE PORCH.

15 A

GLASGOW SCHOOL OF ART: LIBRARY, 1897–99

© Anthony Oliver

At the time of submitting the designs for the School of Art, Mackintosh was a junior architect with the firm Honeyman and Keppie. John Keppie was at first publicly credited with the project. This was in spite of the design having clearly been drawn by Mackintosh and, during the laying of the foundation stone on 25 May 1898, Mackintosh remained very much in the background. By the time of the second phase of building from 1907 to 1909, Mackintosh had become a partner in the firm and his name appeared alongside his plans. The library is quite possibly Mackintosh at his most brilliant. Soaring oak posts support substantial beams holding up the gallery and rhythmically dividing the room into a space of unequalled harmony. There is an undeniable parallel between the physicality of the room and the concept of the tree of knowledge, seen through the heavy oak posts reaching towards the central grouping of 13 lights suspended from the ceiling on tendril-like cords. The symbol of the tree was one that Mackintosh used repeatedly through his career and in all areas of his art.

CREATED
Glasgow

MEDIUM
Interior design

SERIES/PERIOD/ MOVEMENT
Glasgow School of Art

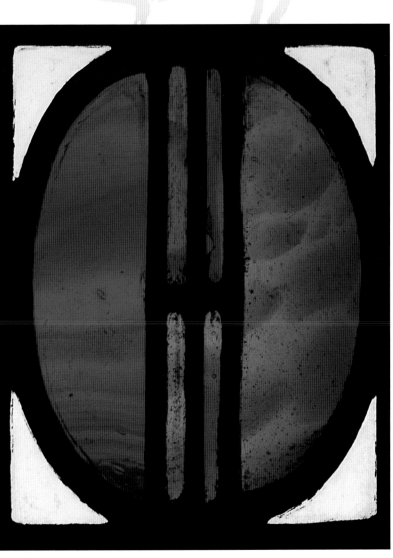

GLASGOW SCHOOL OF ART: GLASS DETAIL, 1896–99

© Anthony Oliver
When designing the School of Art, Mackintosh had an extremely tight budget. Decoration was kept to a minimum and was functional as well as beautiful, as in this glass panel and the ceiling lights in the main picture.

THE ROCKS, (DETAIL) 1927

© The Fine Art Society, London, UK/The Bridgeman Art Library

CREATED
France

MEDIUM
Pencil and
watercolour

**SERIES/PERIOD/
MOVEMENT**
Late period
landscapes

Mackintosh, though much happier in France, still struggled with his self-confidence and his laboriously slow working process was in part a reflection of this. He would continually return to a canvas over a period of time and wrote to Margaret in 1927, 'I find that each of my drawings has something in them, but none of them have everything'.

He was, however, pleased with the finished canvas *The Rocks*, a startling composition combining whimsical natural formations contrasted against the rhythmic regularity of man-made structures. He worked on the picture for a long time, over a month, before being satisfied with it. Correspondence with Margaret affords us a glimpse of his interesting working process: 'I have an insane aptitude for seeing green and putting it down here, there and everywhere the very first thing – this habit complicates every colour scheme... *The Rocks* has some green, and now I see that instead of painting this first I should have painted the grey rock first then I probably would have no real green. But that's one of my minor curses – green-green-green...'.

ROME, ARCH OF TITUS, 1891

© Christie's Images Ltd
Throughout his career, Charles produced many accomplished watercolours. Sadly, they were never exhibited during his life; 30 were shown for the first time in a retrospective exhibition in 1933.

HOUSE FOR AN ART LOVER COMPETITION ENTRY: DESIGN FOR A MUSIC ROOM WITH PANELS BY MARGARET MACDONALD MACKINTOSH, 1901

PUBLISHED IN
Darmstadt

MEDIUM
Colour lithograph

SERIES/PERIOD/ MOVEMENT
House for an Art Lover

Margaret and Charles collaborated on many commissions, Margaret often providing the detailing to fabrics and wall treatments within Charles's design concept. In the music-room plans, the hand of Margaret is distinctive in her use of the unusual linen ladies panels and the elaborate and ornamental piano casing. The decorative nature of Margaret's input was a reflection of the Glasgow style, which the Glasgow School of Art became famous for nurturing. In spite of the excessively decorative

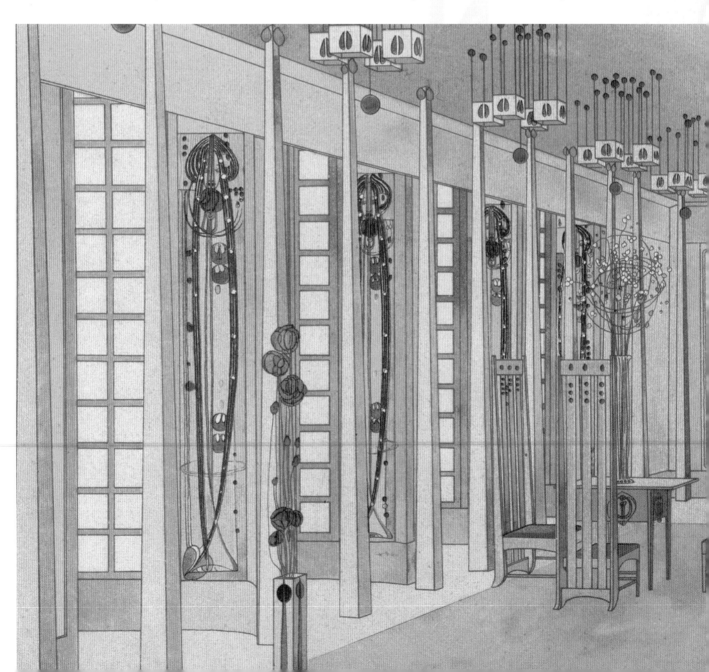

nature of the room, the elegant physical proportions and the lofty sense of verticality preside. The pervading atmosphere is one of sophisticated entertainment, perfectly reflecting the function of the room. The fantastical piano design was based on an organ made for another project that Mackintosh was involved in at Craigie Hall, Glasgow. The music room attracted a great deal of attention and may have inspired the Wärndorfers to commission Mackintosh to design their music room, on which he worked at around the same time as the House for an Art Lover.

OPERA OF THE SEAS, 1903
MARGARET MACDONALD MACKINTOSH
BORN 1864 Tipton, Wolverhampton **DIED** 1933
© The Fine Art Society, London, UK/The Bridgeman Art Library
Although Margaret Macdonald Mackintosh was recognized by her peers as an accomplished artist in her own right, her career was overshadowed by Charles's; she has only recently begun to gain the recognition she deserves.

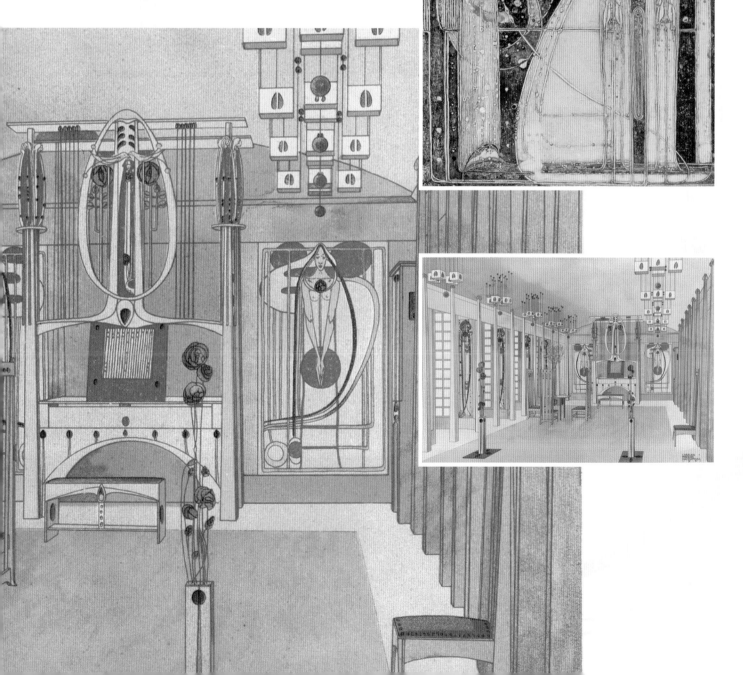

GLASGOW SCHOOL OF ART: THE BOARDROOM, 1897–99

© Anthony Oliver

CREATED
Glasgow

MEDIUM
Interior design

**SERIES/PERIOD/
MOVEMENT**
Glasgow School of Art

The second phase of building from 1907 to 1909 was run under similar financial restraints as the first, against which Mackintosh battled fiercely. On completion, the building was met with the predictable divided criticism. Mackintosh's greatest work was harshly criticized on some fronts, although the governors declared its form was perfectly suited to the function of an art school. The first step towards Modernism, the brilliant synthesis of form and the evocation of a new way forward, all seemed to be largely overlooked. It was perhaps one of the greatest tragedies that Mackintosh never lived to see his masterpiece properly appreciated.

The boardroom, with its innovative steel beams, lofty windows and clean, spare lines, allegedly made the members of the board uncomfortable. More accustomed to the traditional cluttered Victorian interiors, they probably thought the boardroom too sparse and a new boardroom was constructed in a large studio room to the left of the entrance. Panelled and rich in atmosphere and natural colour, the new boardroom has eight carved pilasters topped with Mackintosh's interpretation of an egg and dart moulding, set between narrow Ionic volutes.

GLASGOW SCHOOL OF ART: LIBRARY, 1897–99

© Anthony Oliver

The designs that Mackintosh made for the School of Art managed to fuse a modern, geometric style with academic sobriety, evident in the clean, spare lines and splashes of colour that are a feature of the building.

GLASGOW SCHOOL OF ART: GLASS DETAIL, 1896–99

© Anthony Oliver

CREATED
Glasgow

MEDIUM
Stained glass

SERIES/PERIOD/ MOVEMENT
Glasgow School of Art

Although Mackintosh was dogged by bad luck and poor timing throughout his career, a certain amount of his eventual disenchantment with Glasgow was self-inflicted. By all accounts he was inclined to bouts of temper and petulance, even as a small child, and it seems that his particularly fiery temperament continued on into adulthood. He was described on occasion as being difficult to work with and would frequently change his plans partway through a project. His initial drawings for a commission would identify his intentions, which would then mature and grow throughout the course of the building work. While this practice of a fluid artistic approach towards his architecture undoubtedly produced some of the finest works of the early twentieth century, it could also prove highly irritating to his patrons. The first phase of the Glasgow School of Art, which was to be built under a strict budget, suffered from a large overrun in expenses, causing great consternation amongst the board of commissioners. It was possibly as frustrating for Mackintosh to be so tied financially as it was for the board who saw their budget disappearing.

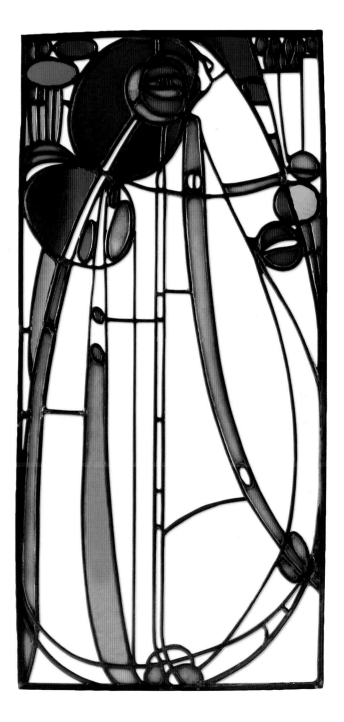

GLASS PANEL, 1902

© Hunterian Museum & Art Gallery, University of Glasgow
Charles Rennie Mackintosh excelled in all areas of art and design; he brought his instantly recognizable style to the furniture, metalwork, textiles, watercolours and stained glass (pictured) that he created.

ROME, ARCH OF TITUS, 1891

© Christie's Images Ltd

CREATED
Rome

MEDIUM
Pencil and
watercolour

**SERIES/PERIOD/
MOVEMENT**
Italian tour

Although Mackintosh was clearly taken with Italy, he was not impervious to the less salubrious side of Italian life. In his diaries he extolled the virtues of the peculiarly 'Italianesque' colours emphasized by the bright sunshine and unlike any he had experienced before, but he was quick to point out that parts of Rome were not dissimilar to the grimy realism of Glasgow's industrial backstreets. He was distracted from his watercolour studies by the thronging Italians and found himself surrounded by Italian peasants, intrigued by the foreigner with the strange accent and the beautiful drawings and hopeful, no doubt, of small handouts. His study of the Arch of Titus reflects the architect in him through the strong lines and accurate perspective. However, the subtle use of colour washes and the strong sense of total design indicate the 'painterly' qualities that would later become his sole artistic focus. When Mackintosh sent a collection of his Italian studies to the Glasgow Students' Club Competition, one of the judges, Sir James Guthrie (1859–1930), on hearing Mackintosh was an architectural student, exclaimed, '... this man ought to be an artist'.

STILL LIFE OF ANEMONES, C. 1915

© Private Collection/The Bridgeman Art Library
Mackintosh's watercolours always began as a pencil sketch and he would sometimes use a colour wash so as not to lose the detail of the original sketch. He then worked them up into sumptuous finished pieces, as here.

INFLUENCES

BLACKTHORN, 1910

© The Fine Art Society, London, UK/The Bridgeman Art Library

CREATED
Chiddingstone, Kent

MEDIUM
Pencil and
watercolour

**SERIES/PERIOD/
MOVEMENT**
Flower studies

After Charles's marriage to Margaret Macdonald in 1900, there was a change in his pattern of sketching. He executed more sketches with a greater degree of finish from one location, with the addition of colour washes and his distinctive signature box. Roger Billcliffe makes the valid point in his book *Mackintosh Watercolours* (1992) that this was due to the addition of a wife. Mackintosh's holidays were now spent in one place for a longer period of time, rather than the pit-stop sketching trips of his bachelor days. On his trip to Chiddingstone, Kent, in 1910, Mackintosh made a number of exquisite watercolour studies of flowers that reflect his interest in Oriental art, especially seen in his painting of *Japonica*, 1910. His inclusion of a signature box, generally providing the date of the picture, the location, title and his initials, is also interesting. Invariably, the initials of Margaret, Herbert MacNair and others would appear alongside his own. Rather than this being an indication of other people contributing to his work, it is thought to represent the people who were present with him while he was sketching.

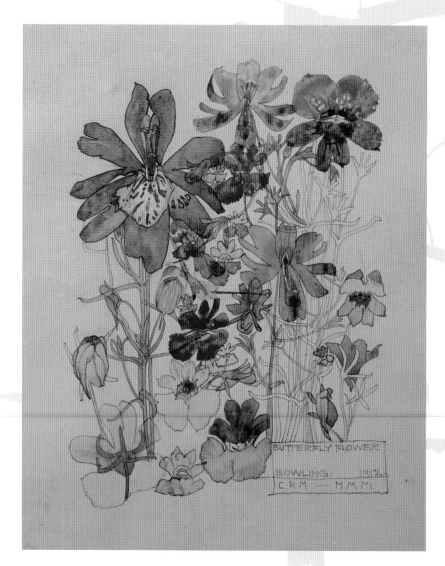

BUTTERFLY FLOWER, 1912

© The Fleming-Wyfold Art Foundation/The Bridgeman Art Library
Mackintosh's floral studies were rather formal. They were always placed centrally on the page and he used a colour wash over his pencil sketch to accentuate the linear form of the subject.

BLACKTHORN
CHIDDINGSTONE
1910   KENT
CRM   MMM

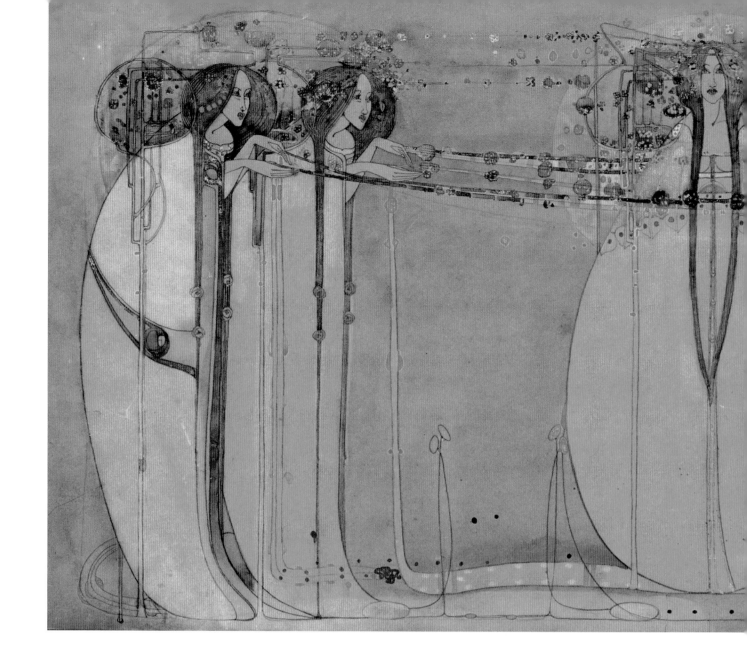

THE MAY QUEEN, 1900

CREATED
Glasgow

MEDIUM
Pencil, watercolour
and body colour,
heightened with silver
on oiled tracing paper

**SERIES/PERIOD/
MOVEMENT**
Gesso panels

Margaret produced *The May Queen* gesso panel to hang in Miss Cranston's Ingram Street Tea Room, opposite a panel by Charles, *The Wassail*. The two panels hung in the White Dining Room in which Charles had created one of his stunning white themes that was evocative of pure light and air. The two panels have strong parallels and were executed in a similar style. Margaret has often been blamed for influencing Mackintosh too much, by her romantic vision and overtly Symbolist expression. Clearly being in such a symbiotic and close relationship, the two would doubtlessly have communicated their individual styles to one another. Their initial individual outlooks could

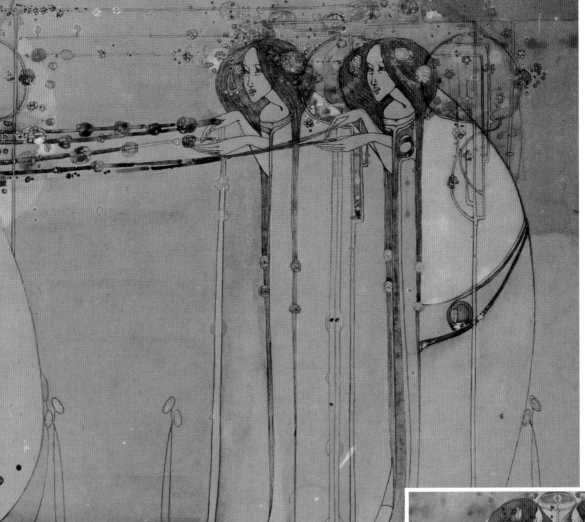

MARGARET
MACDONALD
MACKINTOSH
BORN 1864 Tipton,
Wolverhampton
DIED 1933

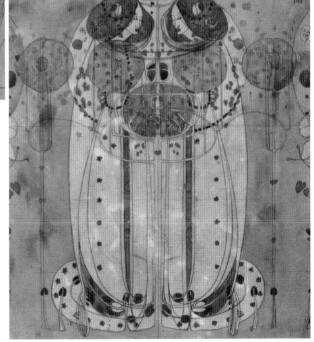

THE WASSAIL (DETAIL), 1900

© Christie's Images Ltd

Both *The Wassail* and *The May Queen* were painted on gesso panels. Gesso, a type of plaster of paris, was first used in the Middle Ages as a preparatory base for oil painting.

not, however, have been more diverse; Charles a man of line and function and Margaret the consummate romantic. It is testament to their relationship that they complemented each other's differences.

Both *The May Queen* and *The Wassail* were strongly three-dimensional in application. The pictures were worked up from a plaster base on coarse canvas and thick string was used to form the outline of the figures. Both pictures had decorative inlaid beads, coloured glass and pieces of metal.

FLORAL AND CHECKED FABRIC DESIGN, C. 1916

© Christie's Images Ltd

CREATED
London

MEDIUM
Pencil and body colour on tracing paper

SERIES/PERIOD/ MOVEMENT
Textile design

Mackintosh's vision had developed from the 'white interior' period of his early designs in Glasgow to a modern concept of design articulated through his bold patterns and bright colours. The fine decorative detailing born from the Scottish equivalent of Art Nouveau and the Four's ethereal mysticism was now replaced with a startlingly vivid new language. Here he combines a stylized organic motif with a strong geometric chequerboard pattern, a contrasting method of expression that he utilized frequently. His use of distorted perspective creates the illusion of an undulating motion through the centre of his design. This further contrasts with the flowers, the organic element, that are totally flat and stylized; as such, he inverts the rationale of organic to geometric. As is the case with innovators of style, Mackintosh's textile designs preceded that which was to come. By the time the bold colours and designs of Art Deco were seen at the Exposition des Arts Décoratifs in Paris in 1925, Mackintosh had turned his back on architecture and designing and was pursuing a career as a watercolourist.

DETAIL OF A DESIGN FOR A PRINTED TEXTILE

© Victoria & Albert Museum, London, UK/The Bridgeman Art Library
After moving to London, both Margaret and Charles began to design textile patterns. The juxtaposition of the organic and geometric shape can be seen here and it was a pairing that cropped up continually throughout Mackintosh's work.

INTERIOR VIEW OF QUEEN'S CROSS CHURCH, GLASGOW, 1897

© Anthony Oliver

Queen's Cross Church, which was turned into the headquarters for the Charles Rennie Mackintosh Society in 1977, is one of the earliest examples of the architect truly synthesizing traditional and modern elements to produce a cohesive expression of his innovative vision. The exterior of the church is at once recognizable by the tower, which is similar to the tower of the Merriot Church in Somerset that Mackintosh had visited and sketched two years previously. The façade looks to the Gothic tradition, especially in the window treatments, but has been expressed with Mackintosh's own language of organic detailing. On the interior, the lofty barrel-vaulted ceiling has been compared by the C. R. Mackintosh Society to that of the Basilica of Vicenza that Mackintosh would have studied during his Italian tour of 1891 and

clearly draws on the influence of Norman Shaw's Harrow Mission Church, Holy Trinity, 1887, situated on the Latimer Road, London. One of the most striking aspects of Queen's Cross is the contrast between the busy exterior of Gothic extraction with the eternally restful and spacious interior presided over by the fantastically unexpected barrel-vaulted roof.

CREATED
Glasgow

MEDIUM
Interior design

SERIES/PERIOD/ MOVEMENT
Early architectural designs

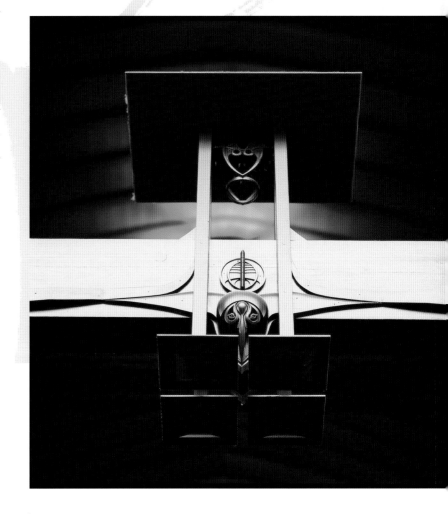

DETAIL OF A BEAM ABOVE THE ALTAR AT QUEEN'S CROSS CHURCH, 1897

© Anthony Oliver
Dotted throughout the church are tree motifs. This was an organic decorative element that Mackintosh returned to again and again in his design work.

OPERA OF THE SEAS, 1903

© The Fine Art Society, London, UK/The Bridgeman Art Library

CREATED
Glasgow

MEDIUM
Gesso panel

**SERIES/PERIOD/
MOVEMENT**
Work of the Four

**MARGARET
MACDONALD
MACKINTOSH
BORN** 1864 Tipton,
Wolverhampton
DIED 1933

This decorative gesso panel by Margaret is typical of the eerily symbolic and mystical works of the Four, especially seen in the work of Margaret and Frances Macdonald. Aubrey Beardsley's powerfully sinister graphic works, most notably his illustrations for *The Yellow Book* first published in 1894 and for Oscar Wilde's *Salome*, were of some consequence in the development of Margaret's style. Beardsley was a keen collector of Japanese art and artefacts, as were Whistler and Rossetti. *In Opera of the Seas* the idiom of Japanese art can clearly be felt and the rhythmic repetition of line and form

suggests Beardsley. Symbolism was a movement that was becoming increasingly popular through Europe at this time and the symbolic content of Margaret's work is significant. The Dutch artist Jan Toorop (1858–1928) was also influential on Margaret's style, with his particular brand of Art Nouveau and Symbolism. However, as much as the young artists drew from the examples of those around them, they also evolved a unique tradition of their own. *Opera of the Seas* is the dreamy, lyrical, melancholic manifestation of Margaret's early work as a designer.

O YE, ALL YE THAT WALK IN WILLOW WOOD, 1903
MARGARET MACDONALD MACKINTOSH
BORN 1864 Tipton, Wolverhampton **DIED** 1933
© Art Gallery & Museum, Kelvingrove, Glasgow, Scotland,
Glasgow City Council (Museums)/The Bridgeman Art Library
Margaret Macdonald Mackintosh was the first artist
to make use of gesso as a medium in its own right;
the technique she used to create these panels is still
not fully understood.

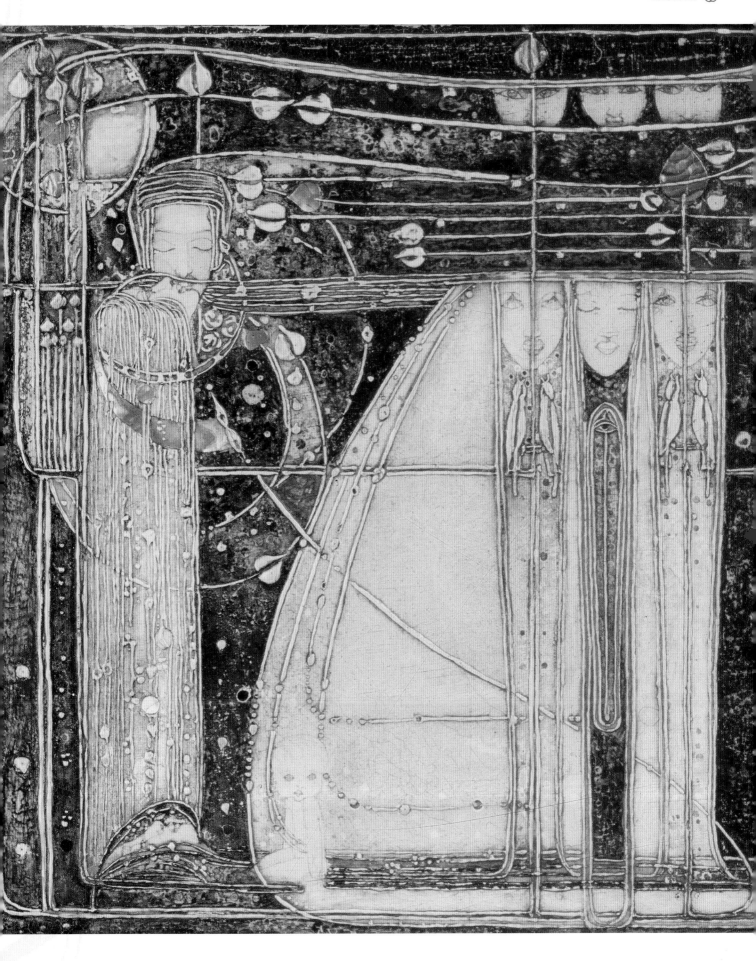

BUTTERFLY FLOWER

BOWLING 1912.

CRM — MMM

BUTTERFLY FLOWER, 1912

By 1912, Mackintosh's career had started its inevitably tragic decline. The glory years faded with the completion of the West Wing of the Glasgow School of Art in 1909 and from that point on his commissions began to dry up. The relationship between Mackintosh and John Keppie had started to deteriorate, a process that resulted in the dissolution of their partnership in 1913. Mackintosh became increasingly depressed, difficult to work with and for, and erratic in his behaviour. His vision of leading the arts forward in a new direction had failed. Where he had hoped for recognition and appreciation for a style born from the Scottish tradition and matured into the realization of modernity, he found criticism, ridicule and total incomprehension.

He continued to work for Miss Cranston, an enlightened and sympathetic patron. In 1912, he designed the White Cockade exhibition café for her and the same year travelled to Bowling, Dumbartonshire, where he made a number of flower studies. The combination of pattern and colour within an organic context seen in his *Butterfly Flower* looks back to the tradition of William Morris and anticipates the bold textile patterns that Mackintosh would design in London.

CREATED
Bowling,
Dumbartonshire

MEDIUM
Watercolour

**SERIES/PERIOD/
MOVEMENT**
Flower studies

THE ROAD THROUGH THE ROCKS, C. 1926–27

The clean lines that Mackintosh employs to depict the fortress shown here are typical of his botanical compositions and of much of his other design and decorative work.

STILL LIFE OF ANEMONES, C. 1915

© Private Collection/The Bridgeman Art Library

CREATED
London

MEDIUM
Watercolour, pencil
and gouache

**SERIES/PERIOD/
MOVEMENT**
Still life

In his 1902 lecture, 'Seemliness', Mackintosh likened art to a flower and rallied his audience to draw from 'flowers that grow from but above the green leaf – flowers that are not dead – are not dying – not artificial – real flowers springing from your own soul – not even cut flowers ...'. The message of truth to oneself, to cultivate an artistic expression born from within in honesty sits beside the obvious literal interpretation of his words. Through his early career he did draw directly from nature. By the time of *Anemones*, he had turned to the depiction of cut flowers. The greater symbolic meaning provides significant content for debate. Did Mackintosh now feel that his artistic expression was

something entirely different? That he could no longer draw from within his soul? Or perhaps the fallen petals of the *Anemones* painting suggest the realization that his artistic vision would not be fulfilled?

This was one of his earliest pictures of cut flowers and was probably painted shortly after his arrival in London. Visible in the painting behind the flowers is a swatch of one of his fabric designs.

BLACKTHORN, 1910

© The Fine Art Society, London,
UK/The Bridgeman Art Library
Mackintosh's botanical studies provide an exciting way to see how the different ways that he experimented with form, colour and pattern, all of which are evident in the two pictures shown here.

DETAIL OF A BEAM ABOVE THE ALTAR AT QUEEN'S CROSS CHURCH, 1897

© Anthony Oliver

Through the treatment of the interior of Queen's Cross, Mackintosh made bold use of the structural elements, leaving the steel crossbeams exposed. In this way, and typical of Mackintosh's holistic approach to his designing, the very structure of the building fills both fundamental and decorative functions. He used ironwork through the whole scheme from the crossbeams to the iron railings, contrasting the natural wood elements with industrial steel. The decorative detailing used is reminiscent of Celtic imagery, something that Mackintosh frequently drew on for inspiration, as seen here, and organic motifs associated with the style of the Four. The tree design carved on the outside of the pulpit was a motif with decorative and symbolic functions for Mackintosh, who returned to it again and again through his architectural designs and decorative work. His use of traditional building elements with industrial materials was another working practice that typifies his modern approach to architecture. By the time he began work on Queen's Cross, he had completed the drawings for the Glasgow School of Art, where his audacious mix of traditional and modern was realized in perfect harmony.

CREATED
Glasgow

MEDIUM
Interior design

SERIES/PERIOD/ MOVEMENT
Early architectural designs

DRAWING ROOM AT THE HILL HOUSE, C. 1903–04

© Anthony Oliver
Mackintosh tried to give everything he designed and created a sense of unity, by using recurring motifs and colour schemes, as with the geometric patterns employed in the drawing room and tree motifs used in the church.

O YE, ALL YE THAT WALK IN WILLOW WOOD, (DETAIL) 1903

© Art Gallery & Museum, Kelvingrove, Glasgow, Scotland,
Glasgow City Council (Museums)/The Bridgeman Art Library

CREATED
Glasgow

MEDIUM
Painted gesso with
twine and coloured
beads

**SERIES/PERIOD/
MOVEMENT**
Gesso panels

**MARGARET
MACDONALD
MACKINTOSH**
BORN 1864 Tipton,
Wolverhampton
DIED 1933

Margaret's beautifully melancholy gesso panel was designed for the Salon De Luxe in the Willow Tea Rooms, the only tea-room commission for which Mackintosh had control over both the exterior and interior renovations. The Salon De Luxe was its sparkling, luxurious heart; brilliant with mirrored leaves and coloured glass, the room emanated light and colour from a hundred different reflections. The entire building was designed to echo the willow tree, a natural and symbolic point of reference for the Mackintoshes. Margaret's panel was the focal point of the room, hanging on the wall opposite the fireplace. This haunting and mystical piece takes its title from a sonnet by Dante Gabriel Rossetti, who was influential on the early development of the style of the Four. The sonnet describes the grief of widowhood, the sadness being so great that 'who so in vain invite your lips to that their unforgotten food ere ye, ere ye again shall see the light'.

The outline of pattern on the panel was created using string and the design embellished with beads and fragments of shell.

SIGN FOR THE WILLOW TEA ROOMS
© Anthony Oliver
Customers who came to the Salon De Luxe, the room that the Mackintoshes created in the Willow Tea Rooms, were so overwhelmed by its magnificence that it is alleged they willingly paid a penny more for their tea.

DETAIL OF A DESIGN FOR A PRINTED TEXTILE

© Victoria & Albert Museum, London, UK/The Bridgeman Art Library

The influence on Mackintosh of the Arts and Crafts movement, spearheaded by William Morris, was significant, especially through the ideas of W. R. Lethaby. Although the Glasgow Four moved away from the Arts and Crafts movement in spirit, the two groups shared a common preoccupation with organic forms and nature as a source of inspiration. The Four were invited to exhibit at the London Arts and Crafts Society Exhibition in 1896, although it proved to be a disaster for them.

The rose motif was one that Mackintosh continued to use through his career, from the early days of the Glasgow Four to the later London years when he made frequent use of the stylized flower form in his textile designs. The design pictured here could have been intended for use as a handkerchief border and demonstrates his synthesis of organic form into a geometric context, a method of designing that he finally evolved through his landscape paintings of southern France. His textile designs with their vibrant colours and strong linear boldness anticipated the emergence of Art Deco, the style of the 1920s and 1930s.

CREATED
Glasgow

MEDIUM
Watercolour

SERIES/PERIOD/MOVEMENT
Textile designs

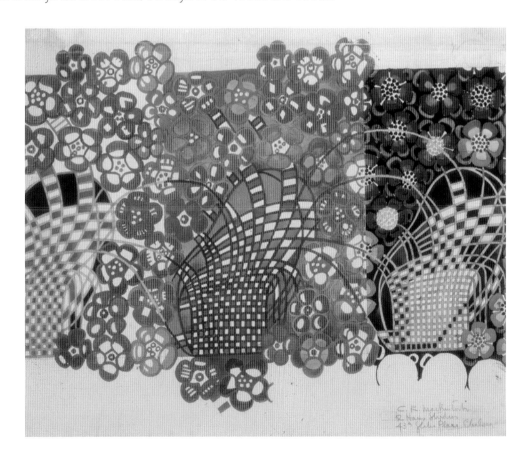

BLUE AND PINK TOBACCO FLOWER DESIGN
© The Fine Art Society, London, UK/The Bridgeman Art Library
Mackintosh's signature stylized, organic-inspired decorative motifs combined with strong angular shapes are brought to the fore in this exuberant textile design.

ROSE MOTIF, THE HILL HOUSE, HELENSBURGH, C. 1902–03

© Anthony Oliver

CREATED
Glasgow

MEDIUM
Stained glass

**SERIES/PERIOD/
MOVEMENT**
Hill House

The evolution of the Glasgow style and that of the Glasgow Four was symptomatic of a widespread rejection of conventional art in favour of a new direction. The exuberance of Art Nouveau, which was so popular on the Continent, had largely been ridiculed in England, a fact that made the style all the more readily accepted into the vocabulary of the forward-thinking young Scots. The simple stylized imagery and use of motifs seen in the increasingly popular Oriental art was also influential in the development of the Glasgow style, which took these elements and translated them into a Scottish idiom. Art was flourishing in Glasgow and not just in painterly circles. There was a huge interest in the decorative arts, metalwork, glasswork and textiles, with much of the renewed enthusiasm attributed to the direction of Francis Newbery.

The Hill House was commissioned by Walter Blackie in 1902 and is considered to be one of the most successful domestic buildings that Mackintosh completed. In contrast to the Scottish vernacular treatment of the exterior, the interior is evocative of Oriental influence and has a continuing theme of the rose motif.

MASTER BEDROOM AT THE HILL HOUSE, C. 1903–04

© Anthony Oliver

The stylized rose that appears in the bedroom, coupled with the geometric forms employed in the furniture perfectly encapsulate Mackintosh's style. The rose shown in the main picture demonstrates the motif's versatility across different media.

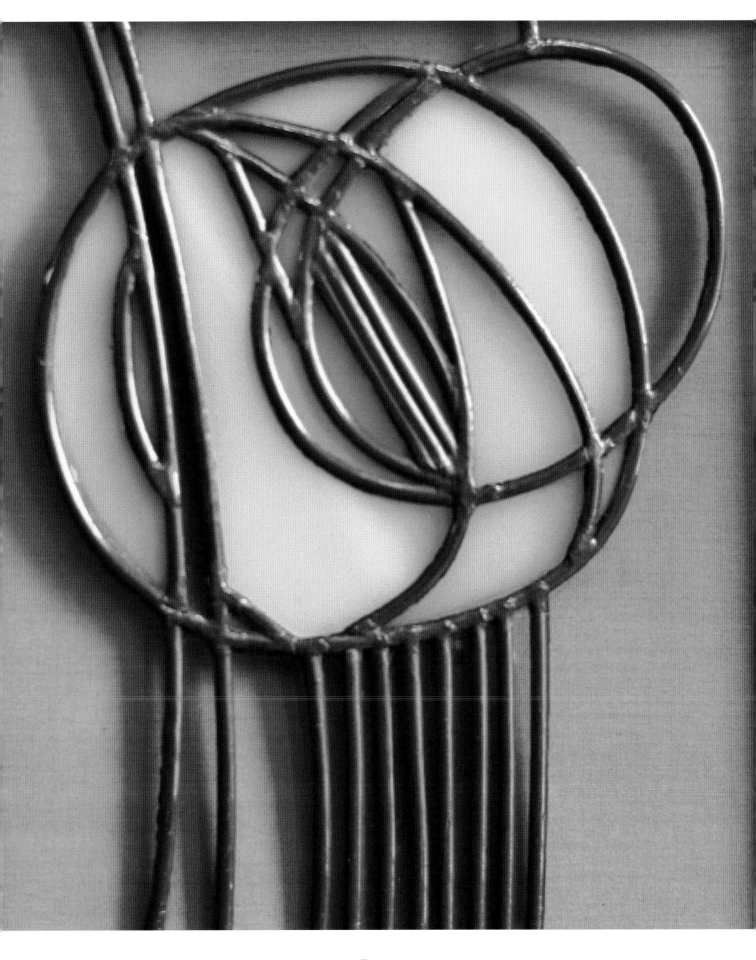

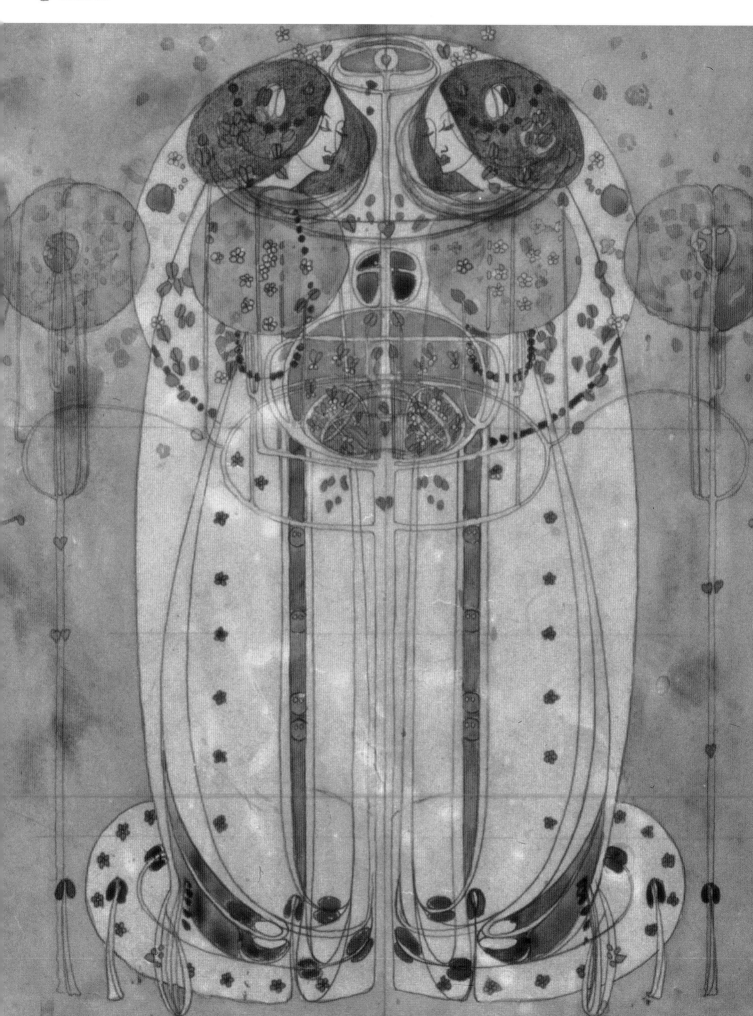

THE WASSAIL (DETAIL), 1900

© Christie's Images Ltd

I n 1900, the Glasgow Four were invited to exhibit at the Eighth Secessionist Exhibition in Vienna, their reputation preceding them on the Continent due to Gleeson White's coverage of their work in *The Studio*. *The Wassail* and *The May Queen* were exhibited in the Scottish Room, facing each other from opposite walls. The room also included furniture from the Mackintoshes' home on Mains Street and a number of watercolours, illustrations and custom-designed furniture. *The Wassail* and *The May Queen* were greatly influential on the Viennese Secessionists, whose work in turn influenced Charles and Margaret. It was an extraordinary phenomenon that two such similar concepts of style had developed independently of each other in two different countries. Gustav Klimt was especially drawn to the Four's style and his *Beethoven Frieze* of 1902 shows clear parallels to the work of Margaret in particular. Josef Hoffman, a founding member of the Secessionists and organizer of the exhibition, became a great supporter of Mackintosh and visited him in Glasgow. The Four's work was criticized by some at the Vienna exhibition, but on the whole, they were received with much more understanding and comprehension than they had been anywhere else.

CREATED
Glasgow

MEDIUM
Watercolour and pencil

SERIES/PERIOD/ MOVEMENT
Gesso panels

DETAIL OF PRELIMINARY DESIGN FOR A DECORATION AT MISS CRANSTON'S BUCHANAN STREET TEA ROOMS, 1896–97

© Glasgow University Art Gallery, Scotland/The Bridgeman Art Library
It has been suggested that the Mackintoshes' work, these pieces in particular, contained mystical symbols from a number of different spritual beliefs. These include the scarab beetle, sacred to Ancient Egyptians and the lotus flower, important in Buddhism.

STYLES & TECHNIQUES

MASTER BEDROOM AT THE HILL HOUSE, C. 1903–04
© Anthony Oliver

CREATED
Glasgow

MEDIUM
Interior design

**SERIES/PERIOD/
MOVEMENT**
Domestic interiors

The master bedroom and the hall were the only two rooms at The Hill House that were furnished exclusively by Mackintosh. In this respect they offer the most unified interior schemes. The master bedroom again demonstrates Mackintosh's technique of delineating separate areas of a room. Here he has created a shallow barrel-vaulted effect in the ceiling that denotes the bed and sleeping area. The curve of the ceiling is reiterated in the curve at the foot of the bed. Mackintosh was always intensely concerned with the manipulation of light and the effect of light on his interiors. Here the small windows allow a soft illumination beyond the level of the sleeping area, while artificial lighting throws a decorative pattern on the walls to the side of the bed. The decorative wall stencilling, which was later covered over, was applied through the room and is contrasted by the dark geometric ladder-back chairs. The overall colour scheme with pastel-pink tones again unifies the room and continues through the rest of the house. In comparison to his later bedroom schemes, this one remains feminine in its delicate handling and pale palette.

DRAWING ROOM AT THE HILL HOUSE, C. 1903–04
© Anthony Oliver
The rooms shown here display a new departure for Mackintosh. Contrasted against the white interiors, he introduces dark pieces, such as the chair in the bedroom and the table in the drawing room.

ARMCHAIR DESIGNED FOR THE BILLIARDS AND SMOKING ROOM AT MISS CRANSTON'S TEA ROOMS, 1898–99

© Christie's Images Ltd

The famous tea rooms of Glasgow were much more than a humble café and the larger ones offered restaurants, smoking rooms, billiard rooms and libraries. They were establishments that ladies could go to unaccompanied without fear of dishonourable recourse and also where gentlemen could congregate in the male-only smoking and billiard areas. Mackintosh, who was keenly aware of feminine and masculine elements in his designs, treated his interiors accordingly. Typically, the masculine areas would invariably be darker and stouter in atmosphere. His armchair is a classic example of this approach. In contrast to the fine and elegant high-backed chairs used in the dining area, his short-backed chair here has a distinctly masculine attitude. The design is sturdy, yet refined and is extraordinarily modern in its geometric form. Mackintosh designed a chair for his own house along similar lines, but with the added feature of small knobs on the rear posts. This commission was independent from Honeyman and Keppie and shows Mackintosh designing without the influence of his employers.

CREATED
Glasgow

MEDIUM
Dark stained oak

SERIES/PERIOD/ MOVEMENT
Chairs

DETAIL OF PRELIMINARY DESIGN FOR A DECORATION AT MISS CRANSTON'S BUCHANAN STREET TEA ROOMS, 1896–97

© Glasgow University Art Gallery, Scotland/The Bridgeman Art Library

Miss Cranston, the tea rooms' proprietor, became one of Mackintosh's most sympathetic patrons. She provided him with numerous commissions throughout his career, culminating in a redesign of her house, Hous'hill.

DESK FOR THE BLUE BEDROOM AT HOUS'HILL, 1904

© The Fine Art Society, London, UK/The Bridgeman Art Library

CREATED
Glasgow

MEDIUM
Wood with glass and
metal inlay

**SERIES/PERIOD/
MOVEMENT**
Domestic interiors

The Blue Bedroom was the first occasion on which Mackintosh did not use a white scheme in a bedroom. The room still retained white walls and ceiling, but all the furniture was either stained dark or was ebonized. Similar to the White Bedroom, he used a predominantly geometric style, with all the furniture being designed around basic square or rectangular forms. His main use of alleviating decorative detail was in stained-glass inlays, such as the stylized organic panel in the desk pictured. This desk is interesting because he designed a very similar one for the White Bedroom, although in that instance he painted the wood with his characteristic white enamel paint. This was one of the last instances that he painted his furniture in this way. In the Blue Bedroom, he concentrated on the beauty of the wood itself, paying great attention to the fine grain and using this as a decorative feature. Little remains of the furniture that he designed for Hous'Hill and the house was later destroyed by a fire before being pulled down by the Glasgow Corporation to make room for a housing estate.

BEDROOM SUITE FOR THE GUEST BEDROOM AT 78 DERNGATE, 1917

© The Fine Art Society, London, UK/The Bridgeman Art Library
The success of the bedroom relies on the beauty of the materials used to create it, as does the desk in the main picture. Mackintosh allowed the wood he chose for the furniture to be the star of the show.

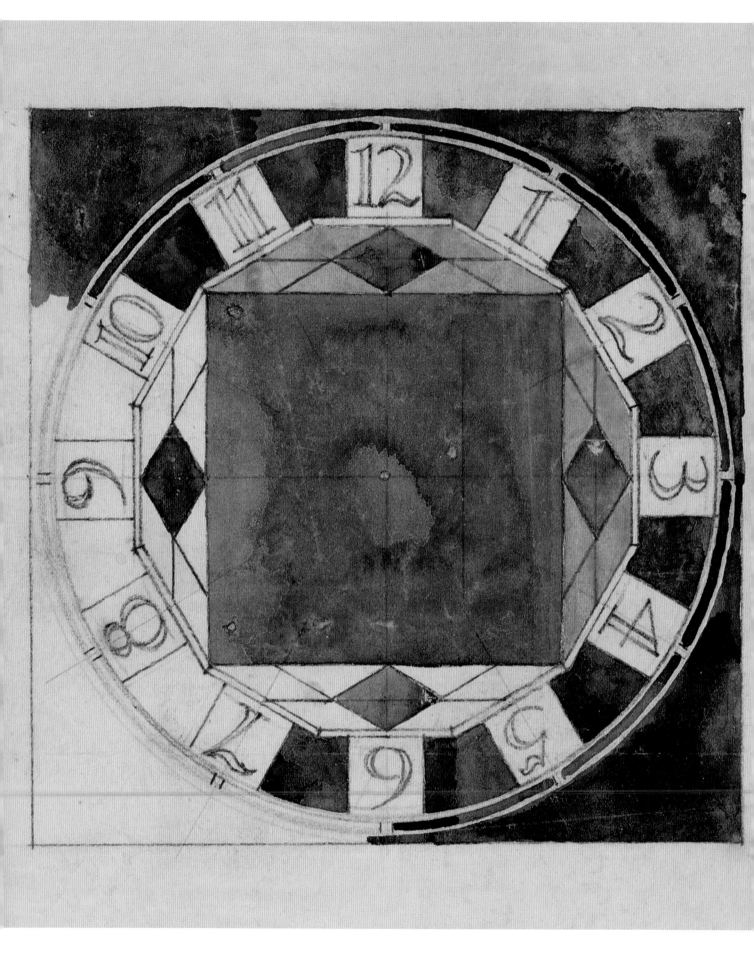

DESIGN FOR A CLOCK FACE FOR W. J. BASSETT-LOWKE, 1917

© Christie's Images Ltd

The design of Mackintosh's clocks is another example of the extraordinary attention to detail that was characteristic of him. It was this attention to detail that made him difficult to work with, but that also ensured his designs were the most impressively cohesive. An amusing indication of the artist's fastidiousness was his insistence that the trees at The Hill House be pruned to the exact shape of the trees in his original architectural drawings and, not content with just that, he apparently rebuked Mrs Blackie for her flower arrangement in the hall at The Hill House because the colours clashed with his interior scheme!

This preliminary drawing for one of the clocks at Derngate expresses the geometry of its intended surroundings and shows Mackintosh developing his colour scheme. The finished clock face was supported by ten columns and the decorative details seen in his drawing were achieved through inlaid ivory and green erinoid. This clock is similar in concept, although more stunning, than one he had designed for The Hill House. Here, the black-lacquered surround vividly contrasts with the ivory and erinoid, creating a dramatic effect.

CREATED
London

MEDIUM
Pencil and watercolour

SERIES/PERIOD/ MOVEMENT
London designs

BEDROOM AT 78 DERNGATE, NORTHAMPTON, 1919

© Anthony Oliver

The geometric forms seen in the bedroom and the clock hint at what Mackintosh was trying to achieve in the house: a sense of unity and a satisfying whole.

EXTERIOR VIEW OF THE HILL HOUSE, C. 1903–04

© Anthony Oliver

CREATED
Glasgow

MEDIUM
Architecture

**SERIES/PERIOD/
MOVEMENT**
Domestic exteriors

Mackintosh's L-shape floor plan allowed the living quarters to sit on one axis, while the service areas were kept separate on their own axis. At The Hill House, the join between them is marked by an unusual round stairwell encased within a turret. This design was unusual in domestic architecture at this time and was further emphasized by the smaller turreted tool shed sitting below it. The exterior looks to the tradition of baronial Scottish architecture in spirit and rendering with the time-worn use of harling (*see* page 118) on the outside walls. The surprising Mackintosh twist, however, is displayed through his use of highly varied window shapes. His exacting approach to detail is demonstrated in his use of the dark grey roofing tiles. During building, a strike at the quarry severely delayed the delivery of the tiles and it was suggested that he look for a different material. None other would do; Mackintosh remained firm and eventually he got his required tiles! Blackie later said of the architect, 'Every detail inside, as well as outside, received his careful, I might say loving, attention'.

FIREPLACE IN THE DRAWING ROOM AT THE HILL HOUSE, C. 1903–04

© Anthony Oliver
Charles's attention to detail was second to none, and frequently caused him problems: budgets over-running, fallings out with patrons; it has been alleged that this fastidiousness could be attributed to borderline autism.

DRAWING ROOM AT THE HILL HOUSE, C. 1903–04

© Anthony Oliver

The drawing room at The Hill House was another one of Mackintosh's 'white rooms'. In his early domestic commissions, he followed a pattern of using predominantly white in bedrooms and drawing rooms and treating dining rooms, libraries and billiard rooms with a darker colour scheme. The drawing room at The Hill House was a particularly fine example of his white rooms and was divided into a summer and winter end. The summer end, pictured, was denoted by a lower ceiling than the rest of the room and comprised a light-filled space surrounding a long horizontal bank of windows. A long window seat with adjacent magazine racks ran the length of the windows and had built-in heating under the seat to ward off the all-pervasive Scottish chill. From the inside looking out, there was a spectacular view down to the Clyde; from the exterior, the little bay was presented as a glazed projection from the main elevation of the house. The curtains would have been designed by Margaret and echoed the shapes of the window panes and the geometric motifs on the wall stencilling.

CREATED
Glasgow

MEDIUM
Interior design

**SERIES/PERIOD/
MOVEMENT**
Domestic interiors

RARE LADDER-BACK CHAIR FOR THE WILLOW TEA ROOMS, 1903

© Christie's Images Ltd
Mackintosh often used opposing elements in his designs, such as masculine and feminine, dark and light, traditional and modern. This was evident in both the Willow Tea Rooms and the drawing room pictured here.

MACKINTOSH

RAILING FROM THE WILLOW TEA ROOMS, GLASGOW, C. 1901–04

© Christie's Images Ltd

CREATED
Glasgow

MEDIUM
Wrought iron and
leaded glass

**SERIES/PERIOD/
MOVEMENT**
Tea room designs

The scheme for the Willow Tea Rooms was the only one for which Mackintosh had total control over both the exterior and interior. He designed the entire building based on a tree-and-leaf motif, of which the latter can clearly be seen in the green glass insets in the wrought-iron railing. The distinctive narrow elegant form of the willow leaf was one that particularly appealed to Mackintosh and here he includes this organic shape within the solid geometric restrictions of the iron surround. Light was especially important to Mackintosh, who made artistic and dramatic use of light sources. His coloured glass insets, seen best in his windows, would bathe his interiors in pools of reflected light, an effect that was systemically created through his absorbing attention to detail. Metal was one of his favourite media, due to its versatility for decorative and structural detail, and he frequently used stained glass and metal together. Glasgow was one of the most progressive cities at this time in the iron industry and, as a result, iron became a popular medium for architects and designers.

INTERIOR OF THE STAIR TOWER OF SCOTLAND STREET SCHOOL, 1904

© Anthony Oliver
Mackintosh was supremely skilled at adding decorative details to his designs without the result looking cumbersome or cluttered. He maintained that no decoration should be without purpose, which is perhaps why his designs appear so seamless.

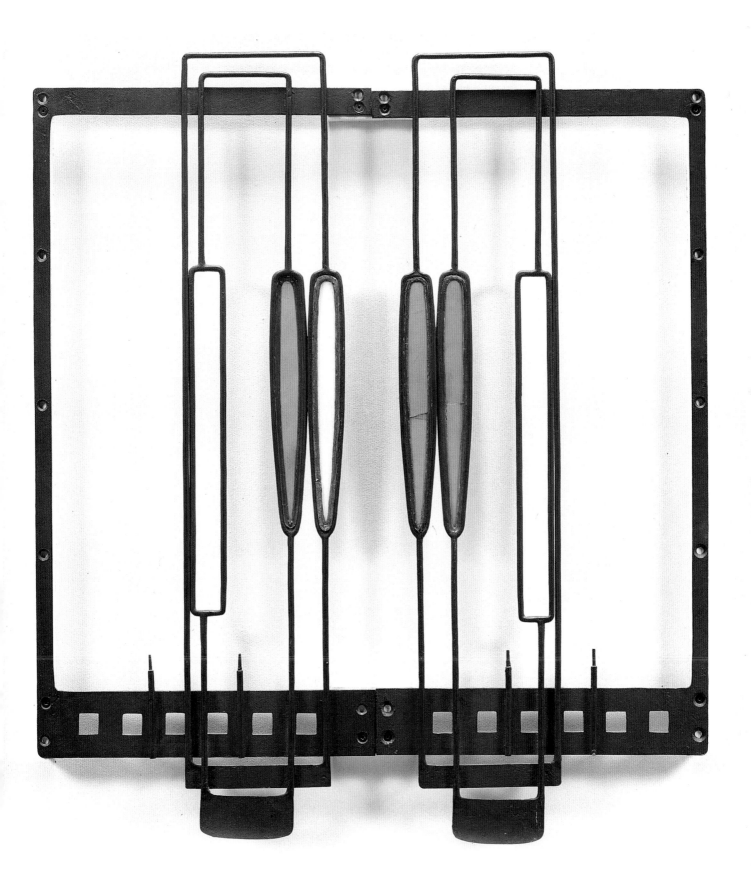

BEDROOM AT 78 DERNGATE, NORTHAMPTON, 1919

© Anthony Oliver

T he guest bedroom at 78 Derngate was one of the most striking interiors that Mackintosh designed. His style of paring down elements to their most minimal was at its most effective here, where the stunning stripes created an arresting visual effect. The furniture he designed for the room was simple in shape and form, the only decorative details being small punched-out squares on the bed baseboards and a narrow frieze of ultramarine squares highlighting the simple furniture design. This detail was similar to the work of Hans Offner, a member of the Viennese School. The white-painted walls and ceiling were striped with black and white, with ultramarine harness-braid edging the design. Thomas Howarth relates an amusing story told by Mr Bassett-Lowke about a visit from his friend George Bernard Shaw. On showing him the bedroom, Bassett-Lowke said, 'I trust the décor will not disturb your sleep', to which Shaw replied, 'No, I always sleep with my eyes closed'.

The techniques and artistic vision that Mackintosh used at Derngate were leading the way towards a new concept of design that was realized through the emergence of Art Deco in the 1920s and 1930s. As with all great artists, Mackintosh was somewhat ahead of his time.

CREATED
London

MEDIUM
Interior design

SERIES/PERIOD/ MOVEMENT
London interiors

DINING ROOM SUITE, C. 1918–19

© The Fine Art Society, London, UK/The Bridgeman Art Library

The dining room suite and the bedroom shown in the main picture reveal a marked move away from the organic, fluid shapes Mackintosh had employed in his earlier work. The pieces here are angular, with no flowing lines to provide a contrast.

MACKINTOSH

EXTERIOR OF WINDYHILL, KILMACOLM, 1901

© Anthony Oliver

CREATED
Glasgow

MEDIUM
Architecture

**SERIES/PERIOD/
MOVEMENT**
Domestic architecture

The exterior of Windyhill demonstrates Mackintosh drawing on the tradition of Scottish vernacular, but translating it into a modern context. He finished the house in a silver-grey rough cast, or harling, which was a traditional method of weatherproofing used since the fifteenth century. The house evokes the spirit of a Scottish farmhouse with the steeply pitched roof and stout chimneys, but the distribution of the windows, reflective of the internal arrangement, was inspiringly modern. The tall and narrow stairwell windows were particularly unusual in domestic architecture at this time and would not become popular for another 20 years or so. The remaining windows are small and irregularly placed with the grey harling extending right into the window openings. In traditional houses of this size and stature the windows would have been dressed with stone sills, lintels and reveals. The unremitting grey of the façade and its monumentality was criticized by local residents who referred to the house as a 'barracks'. In view of this, the owners later added shutters to relieve the oppressiveness of the external features.

EXTERIOR VIEW OF THE HILL HOUSE, C. 1903–04

© The Fine Art Society, London, UK/The Bridgeman Art Library
The foreboding, angular exteriors of both these houses serve to emphasize their interiors, which were meticulously decorated, smooth and comfortable. This was an intentional juxtaposition by Mackintosh: one would move from the outside world to a safe, warm haven.

FABRIC DESIGN, 1916

© Christie's Images Ltd

The surviving sketches for fabric designs that Mackintosh made during his London years offer a fascinating look at the artist's working process. Here, for example, he was experimenting with various colours, building up his pattern in different areas so that he could compare the aesthetic effect. This drawing also demonstrates his technique of using a pencil-drawn grid on which to base his pattern. This grid technique was seen many times in his drawings, as was his use of varying papers and working materials, although he favoured tracing paper and a combination of watercolour and pencil or ink. His interest in different media was further explored through his use of coloured glass, inlaid precious materials and metal panels as decorative details. This sketch is similar to the designs that he created while working at 78 Derngate for W. J. Bassett-Lowke. He produced a series of stunningly modern interior schemes for Bassett-Lowke that centred on bold geometric patterns of triangles and squares. The use of the triangle as a motif was one that the Viennese designer Josef Urban greatly favoured.

CREATED
London

MEDIUM
Pencil and body colour on oiled tracing paper

SERIES/PERIOD/ MOVEMENT
London textile designs

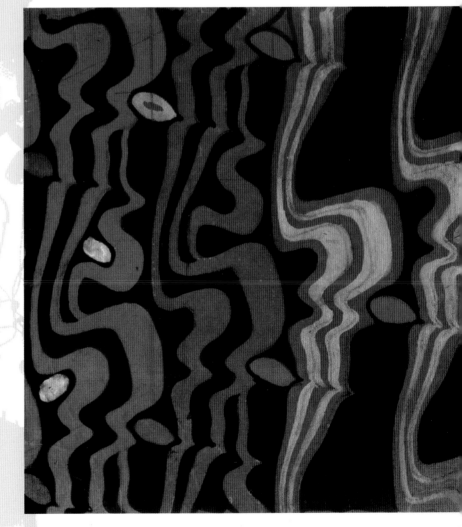

TEXTILE DESIGN

© Christie's Images Ltd
These two samples of Mackintosh's textiles typify his whole style. One displays the organic lines seen in so much of his early work, while the other geometric pattern is believed by many to herald the Art Deco movement.

AUTHOR BIOGRAPHIES

TAMSIN PICKERAL (AUTHOR)

Tamsin Pickeral has studied Art and History of Art since she was child, and lived for some time in Italy furthering her appreciation of the subject. She has travelled extensively throughout her life, and has recently returned to the UK after nine years spent living an unusual life on a cattle ranch in the US. She now resides in Norfolk with her husband, where she continues to write about art and horses, two of her favourite subjects.

ANNE ELLIS (FOREWORD)

Anne Elllis is an architectural historian with a classical background, having first lectured on classical civilization then architecture and design at Glasgow University. She still does a few lectures every year for the university's History of Art Department, in between writing articles and reviewing books. For 12 years she was the curator at The Hill House, Helensburgh, designed by Mackintosh, and describes her time there as 'absolute heaven – like living inside a work of art!'. More recently an interest in broadcasting has developed into a regular slot presenting The Arts Show for Radio Scotland.

PICTURE CREDITS:

Front cover: Charles Rennie Mackintosh, Glass Panel, 1902, © Hunterian Museum & Art Gallery, University of Glasgow

Page 1: Charles Rennie Mackintosh, Detail from an ebonized mahogany writing cabinet, 1904, © Christie's Images Ltd

Page 3: Charles Rennie Mackintosh, Rose Motif, The Hill House, Helensburgh, c. 1902–03, © Anthony Oliver

Page 4 and 128: Charles Rennie Mackintosh, *The Wassail* (detail), 1900, © Christie's Images Ltd

Page 8: Margaret Macdonald Mackintosh, *The May Queen*, 1900, © Christie's Images Ltd

Page 9: Charles Rennie Mackintosh, Glass Panel, 1902, © Hunterian Museum & Art Gallery, University of Glasgow

Page 10: Charles Rennie Mackintosh, Detail of a beam above the altar at Queen's Cross Church, 1897, © Anthony Oliver

Page 11: Charles Rennie Mackintosh, Glasgow School of Art: the boardroom, 1897–99, © Anthony Oliver

Page 12 and 124: Charles Rennie Mackintosh, Domino Clock, 1917, © Art Gallery & Museum, Kelvingrove, Glasgow, Scotland, Glasgow City Council/The Bridgeman Art Library

Page 13: Margaret Macdonald Mackintosh, The White Cockade: illustration for a menu, 1911, © Christie's Images Ltd

Page 14: Charles Rennie Mackintosh, *The Road Through the Rocks*, c. 1926–27, © Christie's Images Ltd

Page 15: Charles Rennie Mackintosh, *Butterfly Flower*, 1912, © The Fleming-Wyfold Art Foundation/The Bridgeman Art Library

Page 16: Charles Rennie Mackintosh, Desk for the Blue Bedroom at Hous'Hill, 1904, © The Fine Art Society, London, UK/The Bridgeman Art Library

Page 17: Charles Rennie Mackintosh, Detail of preliminary design for a decoraion at Miss Cranston's Buchanan Street Tea Rooms, 1896–97, © Glasgow University Art Gallery, Scotland/The Bridgeman Art Library

Back cover: Top: House for an Art Lover competition entry: design for a music room with panels by Margaret Macdonald Mackintosh, 1901, © The Stapleton Collection/The Bridgeman Art Library. Left: Rare ladder-back chair for the Willow Tea Rooms, 1903, © Christie's Images Ltd. Right: Cabinet made for 14 Kingsborough Gardens, Glasgow, 1902, © The Fine Art Society, London, UK/The Bridgeman Art Library

FURTHER READING

With thanks to the Hunterian Museum, Glasgow, and the Charles Rennie Mackintosh Society

Benton, C., *Art Deco 1910–1939*, V&A Publications, 2003

Billcliffe, R. (ed.), *Mackintosh Textile Designs*, John Murray,1982

Billcliffe, R., *Mackintosh Furniture*, Cameron and Hollis, 1990

Billcliffe, R., *Mackintosh Watercolours*, John Murray, 1992

Brandstätter, C., *Wonderful Wiener Werkstätte: Design in Vienna 1903–1932*, Thames and Hudson, 2003

Buchanan, W., *Mackintosh's Masterwork: Charles Rennie Mackintosh & the Glasgow School of Art*, Chronicle Books, 1989

Burkhauser, J. (ed.), *Glasgow Girls: Women in Art and Design, 1880–1920*, Canongate Books Ltd, 1990

Crawford, A., *Charles Rennie Mackintosh*, Thames and Hudson Ltd, 1995

Duncan, A., *Art Nouveau Furniture*, Thames and Hudson Ltd, 1982

Duncan, A., *Art Nouveau*, Thames and Hudson Ltd, 1994

Hackney, F. & I., *Charles Rennie Mackintosh*, Apple Press, 1989

Hiesinger, K. B. (ed.), *Art Nouveau in Munich: Masters of the Jugendstil*, Prestel Verlag, 1988

Howarth, T., *Charles Rennie Mackintosh and the Modern Movement*, Routledge, 1977

Jones, A., *Charles Rennie Mackintosh*, Smithmark Publications, 1996

Kaplan, W, (ed.), *Charles Rennie Mackintosh*, Abbeville Press, 1996

Kinchin, P., *Tea and Taste: The Glasgow Tea Rooms 1875–1975*, White Cockade Publishing, 1991

Koizumi, K., *Traditional Japanese Furniture*, Kodansha Europe, 1995

MacLeod, R., *Charles Rennie Mackintosh: Art and Artist*, E. P. Dutton, 1983

Parry, L. (ed.), *William Morris*, Philip Wilson Publishers, 1996

Poulson, C., *William Morris*, Apple Press, 1989

Rennhofer, M., *Koloman Moser: Master of Viennese Modernism*, Thames and Hudson Ltd, 2002

Robertson, P. (ed.), *Charles Rennie Mackintosh: The Architectural Papers*, White Cockade Publishing, 1990

Robertson, P., *Charles Rennie Mackintosh: Art is a Flower*, Pavilion Books Ltd, 1995

Samuels, C., *Art Deco Textiles*, V&A Publications, 2003

Schweiger, W. J., *Wiener Werkstätte: Design in Vienna, 1903–32*, Thames and Hudson Ltd, 1990

Soros, S. W., *E. W. Godwin: Aesthetic Movement Architect and Designer*, Yale University Press, 1999

Steele, J., *Charles Rennie Mackintosh: Synthesis in Form*, Wiley-Academy, 1994

Toman, R. (ed.), *Vienna: Art and Architecture*, Konemann UK Ltd, 1999

Vergo, P., *Art in Vienna, 1898-1918: Klimt, Schiele and Their Contemporaries*, Phaidon Press, 1993

Wilhide, E., *Mackintosh Style: Design and Décor*, Chronicle Books, 1998

INDEX BY WORK

Works are by Charles Rennie Mackintosh
unless otherwise specified

Arch of Titus, Rome 64, 73
Argyle Street Tea Rooms
    Armchair designed for the billiards and smoking room 53, 104

Blackthorn 77, 88
Blue and pink tobacco flower design 95
Buchanan Street Tea Rooms
    Preliminary design for a mural decoration 51, 99, 105
Butterfly Flower 76, 86

Conversazione Programme 27

78 Derngate, Northampton
    Bedroom 109, 116
    Bedroom suite for the guest bedroom 106
    Design for a clock face 20, 108
Design for a printed textile 80, 94
Detail from an ebonized mahogany
    writing cabinet 23, 33
Dining room suite 25, 117
Domino Clock 21, 36

Fabric design, 1916 39, 120
Floral and checked fabric design 81

Glasgow School of Art
    The Boardroom 60, 69
    Director's Room 28, 34
    Glass Detail 63, 70
    Library 62, 68
    View of a Studio (photograph) 26
    Views of the Exterior 29
Glass Panel, 1902 30, 71

The Hill House, Helensburgh
    Drawing room 91, 102, 112
    Exterior view 111, 118
    Fireplace in the drawing room 110
    Master bedroom 96, 103
    Rose motif 45, 97
House for an Art Lover competition
    Design for a dining room 58
    Design for a Music Room (with Margaret
        Macdonald Mackintosh) 59, 66
Hous'hill
    Desk for the blue bedroom 107

Ingram Street Tea Rooms
    Designs for writing desks 46

14 Kingsborough Gardens
    Cabinet 22

The May Queen (Margaret Macdonald Mackintosh) 32, 78

Oh Ye, All Ye That Walk in Willow Wood (Margaret
    Macdonald Mackintosh) 84, 93
Opera of the Seas (Margaret Macdonald Mackintosh) 67, 85

Palermo Cathedral, study of an entrance porch 61

Queen's Cross Church
    Detail of a beam above the altar 83, 90
    Interior view 82

The Road Through the Rocks 57, 87
The Rocks 56, 65

Scotland Street School
    Interior of the stair tower 44, 114
Still Life of Anemones 72, 89

Table with mother-of-pearl inlay 24, 37
Textile Design 121

Washstand c. 1917 38
The Wassail 79, 98
The White Cockade
    Illustration for a menu 47, 50
Willow Tea Rooms
    Glass panel 31
    Railing 42, 115
    Rare Ladder-Back Chair 48, 113
    Settle from the Dug Out 49, 52
    Sign for 43, 92
Windyhill House, Kilmacolm
    Exterior 35, 119

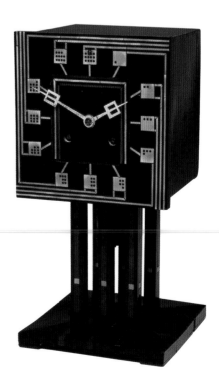

GENERAL INDEX

Aestheticism 16
America 9
architecture 10, 12, 14, 15, 16, 17, 80
 beam above the altar, Queen's Cross Church 83, 90–1
 Glasgow School of Art 12–13, 16, 66, 91
 Hill House, The 9, 16, 32
 Little Hedgecourt, Sussex 24
 Queen's Cross Church, 1897, 82–3
 Scotland Street School, 1904 44–5, 114
 Willow Tea Room 42
 Windyhill House 32
Argyle Street 105
armchairs, 1898-99 53, 104–5
Art Deco 12, 80, 95, 117, 121
art galleries 53
Art Nouveau 9, 28, 53, 58, 80, 96
Arts and Crafts 59, 95
Arts and Crafts Society Exhibition, 1896 28, 95

Basilica, Vicenza 83
Bassett-Lowke, W. J. 20, 24, 109, 116, 121
 New Ways 13
beam above the altar, Queen's Cross Church 83, 90–1
Beardsley, Aubrey 84
Behrens, Peter 13
Billcliffe, Roger *Mackintosh Watercolours* 76
billiard rooms 49
 armchairs 53, 104–5
Blackie, Mrs 109
Blackie, Walter 9, 32, 96, 110
Blackthorn, 1910 76–7, 88
Blue Bedroom, Hous'Hill, 1904 106
Bowling, Dumbartonshire 87
Bridge of Weir 23
Buchanan Street Tea Rooms 50
 mural design, 1896-97 50–1, 99, 105
Butterfly Flower, 1912 76, 86–7

cabinets 22–3, 32–3
Celtic imagery 91
chairs 31
 armchairs, 1898-99 53, 104–5
 ladder-back chair, 1903 48–9, 113
Charles Rennie Mackintosh Society 83
Chiddingstone, Kent 76
Chinese Room 46
clock designs 20–1, 36, 108–9
Cloister Room 46
Continent 9, 17, 28, 31, 96
Conversazione Programme 26–7
Craigie Hall, Glasgow 67
Cranston, Catherine 10, 32, 78, 87
 Buchanan Street Tea Rooms 50
 Ingram Street Tea Room 78
 White Cockade 46
 Willow Tea Rooms 49, 53
cutlery 10

Darmstadt, Hesse 59
Davidson, William, Junior 32, 118
decorative arts 96
Dekorative Kunst 23
Derngate 10, 36, 121
 bedroom suite for guest bedroom, 1917 106
 bedroom, 1919 109, 116–17
 design for a clock face, 1917 108–9
 dining room suite 24–5, 117
 Domino Clock, 1917 20–1, 36
Design for a Dining Room, 1901 58–9
Design for a Music Room with Panels, 1901 59, 66–7
desk for Blue Bedroom, Hous'Hill, 1904 106–7
Deutsche Kunst und Dekoration 23
dining room suite, 1918 24–5, 117
Domino Clock, 1917 20–1, 36
Dug Out 20
 settle 49, 52–3

Edward VII 46
Eighth Secessionist Exhibition, 1900 31, 99
England 28, 96
erinoid 20, 105
Exposition des Arts Décoratifs, 1925 80

fabric design, 1916 39, 120–1
Fetges 56
fireplaces 23
 Dug Out 53
 Hill House, The 110
First World War 10, 17, 53
floral and checked fabric design, 1916 80–1
France 56, 95
Franklin, Harry 24
furniture 10, 13, 17, 39, 71
 armchairs, 1898-99 53, 104–5
 bedroom suite for guest bedroom, 1917 106
 cabinets 22–3, 32–3
 chairs 31
 design for a clock face, 1917 108–9
 desk for Blue Bedroom, Hous'Hill, 1904 106–7
 dining room suite 24–5, 117
 Domino Clock, 1917 20–1, 36
 ladder-back chair, 1903 48–9, 113
 settle 49, 52–3
 table with mother of pearl inlay, 1918 24, 36–7
 washstand, 1917 38–9
 writing desks 17, 32, 46

Gate Lodge, Auchenbothie 23
Gaudi, Antonio 9
geometric patterns 23, 36, 45, 80, 91, 109, 113, 121
George V 46
gesamtkunstwerk 9
gesso 78, 79, 84, 92
Glasgow 9, 15, 17, 50, 72
 tea rooms 10, 42, 50, 53, 105
Glasgow Architectural Association 26–7
Glasgow Boys 53

Glasgow Corporation 106
Glasgow Four 14–15, 16, 17, 26, 27
    Arts and Crafts Society Exhibition, 1896 28, 95
    Eighth Secessionist Exhibition, 1900 99
    style 80, 84, 91, 92, 95, 96
    see Macdonald, Frances
    see Macdonald, Margaret
    see Mackintosh, Charles Rennie
    see MacNair, Herbert
Glasgow International Exhibition, 1911 46
Glasgow School of Art 12–13, 16, 66, 91
    Boardroom, 1897-99 60, 68–9
    Director's Room, 1897-99 28, 34–5
    glass detail, 1896-99 63, 70–1
    Library, 1897-99 62–3, 68
    Newbery, Francis 26, 28
    view of a studio 26
    view of the exterior, built 1897-99 28–9
    West Wing 87
Glasgow Students' Club Competition 72
Glasgow style 8, 26, 66, 96
glass 23, 45, 96
    glass detail, 1896-99 63, 70–1
    glass panel, 1902 30–1, 71
    stained glass 32, 71, 106, 115
Gothic 83
Guimard, Hector 9
Guthrie, Sir James 72

harling 110, 118
Harrow Mission Church, Holy Trinity, London 83
Helensburgh 32, 45, 96
Hill House, The 9, 16, 32, 36, 109
    drawing room, 1903-04 91, 102, 110, 112–13
    exterior view 110–11, 118
    fireplace in the drawing room 110
    master bedroom, 1903-04 96, 102–3
    rose motif 45, 96–7
    writing desks, 1904 32
Hoffman, Josef 9, 10, 99
Honeyman and Keppie 28, 63, 105
Hoppé, E. O. 24
Horta, Victor 9
Hous'Hill, Blue Bedroom 106
House for an Art Lover Competition 58, 59, 67
Howarth, Thomas 39, 117
Hunterian Gallery, Glasgow 24

Ideal Home 10
Industrial Revolution 9
Ingram Street Tea Rooms 46
    May Queen, The 32, 78–9
    Wassail, The 78, 79, 98–9
    White Dining Room 78
    writing desks, 1909 46
inlays 20, 24, 32, 36–7, 39, 106, 109
interior design 10, 12–13, 80
    Blue Bedroom, Hous'Hill 106
    Boardroom, Glasgow School of Art, 1897-99 60, 68–9
    Buchanan Street Tea Rooms 50
    Director's Room, Glasgow School of Art 28, 34–5
    drawing room, The Hill House 91, 102, 110, 112–13
    Dug Out 53
    glass panel, 1902 30–1, 71
    Ingram Street Tea Rooms 46, 78
    Kingsborough Gardens 23

Library, Glasgow School of Art, 1897-99 62–3, 68
    master bedroom, The Hill House 96, 102–3
    Rose Boudoir 31
    Salon De Luxe 42, 49, 53, 92
    White Cockade 46–7, 87
    Willow Tea Rooms 49
International Exhibition of Modern Decorative Art, 1902 31
Italy 56, 60, 72, 83
ivory 32, 109

Japanese design 24, 84
Japonica, 1910 76

Keppie, Jessie 15
Keppie, John 15, 63, 87
Kilmalcolm 23, 118
Kingsborough Gardens, Glasgow 23
    cabinet 22–3
Klimt, Gustav 9
    Beethoven Frieze, 1902 99

ladies rooms 49
lectures 26–7
    Seemliness 23, 88
Lethaby, W. R. 95
libraries 105
light fittings 10, 58
Little Hedgecourt, Sussex 24
Liverpool Cathedral 32
Lloyd George, David 46
London 15, 28, 39, 88, 95, 121
London Salon of the Independents 36
Lutyens, Sir Edwin 10

Macdonald, Frances 14, 16, 26, 84
Macdonald, Margaret 14, 15–16, 26, 99
    Design for a Music Room with Panels 59, 66–7
    Hill House, The 113
    May Queen, The 32, 78–9
    music salon 31
    O Ye, All Ye that Walk in Willow Wood 84, 92–3
    Opera of the Seas, 1903 67, 84–5
    painting 56, 64, 76
    parties 15–16, 39
    Plough 36
    Rose Boudoir 31
    White Cockade 46–7, 50
Mackintosh House, Hunterian Gallery 24
Mackintosh, Charles Rennie 8–11
    architectural work 16–17
    Glasgow Four 14–15
    marriage 15–16
    personal vision 12–14
MacNair, Herbert 14, 16, 26, 76
May Queen, The, 1900 32, 78–9, 99
Merriot Church, Somerset 83
metalwork 71, 96
    railing, 1901-04 42, 114–15
Modernism 12, 16, 31, 36, 39
    Glasgow School of Art 28, 68
    Scotland Street School 45
    Willow Tea Rooms 42
Morris, Margaret 39
Morris, William 87, 95
Moscow Exhibition of Modern Art and Design 32
mother-of-pearl 24, 32, 36–7, 39

motifs 44, 58, 95
   domino motif 20
   geometric patterns 23, 45, 80, 91, 113, 121
   rose motif 23, 45, 95, 96–7
   trees 42, 63, 83, 91, 114
mural design 50–1
music salon 31
Muthesius, Hermann *The English House* 10

National Exhibition of Palermo, 1891-92 60
New Ways 13
Newbery, Francis 14, 23, 96
   Glasgow School of Art 26, 28
Northampton 10, 109, 117

O Ye, All Ye that Walk in Willow Wood 84, 92–3
oak 23, 63
Offner, Hans 117
Opera of the Seas, 1903 67, 84–5
Oriental art 45, 76, 96

Palermo, Sicily 60
Paris 36, 80
pear-wood 32
Plough 24, 36
Port Vendres, France 56
Post-Impressionism 46

Queen's Cross Church, Glasgow, 1897 82–3

railing, 1901-04 42, 114–15
restaurants 46, 49, 105
Road Through the Rocks, The, 1926-27 56–7, 87
Rocks, The, 1927 56, 64–5
Rome, Arch of Titus, 1891 64, 72–3
Rose Boudoir 31
rose motif 23, 95
   Hill House, The 45, 96–7
Rossetti, Dante Gabriel 84, 92
Rowat, Mrs 23

Salome 84
Salon De Luxe 42, 49, 53, 92
Salon des Indépendants, Paris 36
Sauchiehall Street, Glasgow 42, 49
Scotland 12, 26, 87, 96, 118
Scotland Street School, 1904 44–5, 114
Scott, Baillie 58–9
Scottish Baronial architecture 110
Scottish vernacular architecture 35, 96, 118
Secessionists 31, 99
settle 49, 52–3
Shaw, George Bernard 117
Shaw, Norman 83
Sicily 60
silver leaf 23
sketching 72, 76
smoking rooms 49
   armchairs 53, 104–5
Spain 56
Spanish Farm 56
stained glass 32, 71, 106, 115
stencilling 23, 113
Still Life of Anemones, 1915 72, 88–9
Studio, The 10, 28, 50, 99

Study of an Entrance Porch, Palermo Cathedral, 1891 60–1
Symbolism 16, 78, 84

table with mother of pearl inlay, 1918 24, 36–7
tea rooms 10, 42, 50, 53, 105
   Buchanan Street Tea Rooms 50–1, 99, 105
   Ingram Street Tea Rooms 32, 46, 78–9, 98–9
   Willow Tea Rooms 20, 31, 32, 42–3, 48–9, 53, 92, 113, 114–15
textiles 10, 13, 39, 71, 87, 96
   design for a printed textile 80, 94–5
   fabric design, 1916 39, 120–1
   floral and checked fabric design, 1916 80–1
   textile design 121
Tiffany, Louis Comfort 9
Todd, Alfred 23
Toorop, Jan 84
trees 42, 63, 83, 91, 114
Turin 31

Urban, Josef 121

Victoriana 9, 12, 13
Vienna 17, 31, 99
Viennese School 117
Voysey, Charles 10

Walberswick 15
Walton, George 50
Wärndorfer, Fritz 31, 67
washstand, 1917 38–9
Wassail, The 1900 78, 79, 98–9
watercolours 10, 13–14, 71, 80
   Blackthorn, 1910 76–7, 88
   Butterfly Flower, 1912 76, 86–7
   Design for a Dining Room, 1901 58–9
   Design for a Music Room with Panels, 1901 59, 66–7
   Fetges 56
   Japonica, 1910 76
   Road Through the Rocks, The, 1926-27 56–7, 87
   Rocks, The, 1927 56, 64–5
   Rome, Arch of Titus, 1891 64, 72–3
   Spanish Farm 56
   Still Life of Anemones, 1915 72, 88–9
   Study of an Entrance Porch, Palermo Cathedral, 1891 60–1
Whistler, James Abbott McNeill 84
White Cockade 46–7, 50, 87
white rooms 12, 35, 80, 113
   White Bedroom 106
   White Dining Room 78
White, Gleeson 10, 28, 50, 99
Wilde, Oscar 84
Willow Tea Rooms 20, 32
   Dug Out 20
   glass panel 31
   ladder-back chair, 1903 48–9, 113
   railing, 1901-04 42, 114–15
   Salon De Luxe 42, 49, 53, 92
   sign 42–3, 92
Windyhill House, Kilmalcolm, 1901 32
   exterior 118–19
Wright, Frank Lloyd 9, 10
writing desks 17, 32, 46, 106–7

Yellow Book, The 84

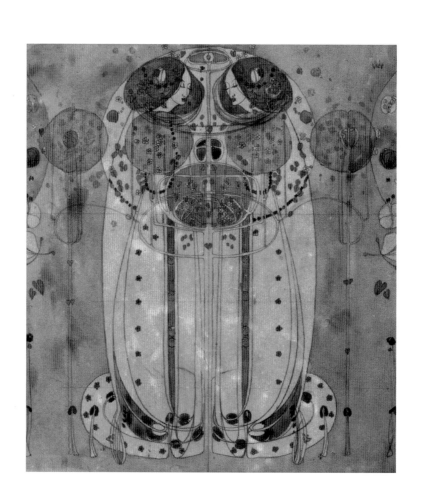